GO BIG
or Go Home!
Examining the Exceptional

Other Books by Jarvis L. Collier

Biblical Challenges for Christian Singles

The Preacher's Journey

A Passion for Excellence

Seeking the Kingdom

Living in the Faith Dimension

A Time to Speak!

Whatever Happened to Christian Evangelism?

Faith of Our Fathers: Spiritual Legacies

Go Big or Go Home!
Examining the Exceptional

Jarvis L. Collier

Townsend Press

Sunday School Publishing Board
Nashville, Tennessee

Scripture quotations are from the New American Standard Bible®. Copyright © 1960, 1962, 1963, 1968, 1971, 1972, 1973, 1975, 1977, 1995 by The Lockman Foundation. Used by permission. (www.Lockman.org)

Published by Townsend Press
Nashville, Tennessee
© 2017 by Jarvis L. Collier

All rights reserved.
Printed in the United States of America.

ISBN 978-1-939225-38-2

**To Mr. Douglas and Mrs. Meryle Carter
Los Angeles, CA**

When I was a college student four decades ago they saw, shared with, and substantively supported me. I pray this book serves as a return on their many investments in my life and ministry for Christ!

Table of Contents

Acknowledgments ix

Introduction 1

Chapter 1   The "Go Big" Way 3

Chapter 2   Sad Tales of "Go Home" 16

Chapter 3   Go Big: Assessing Knowledge and Skill Sets 28

Chapter 4   Go Big: Self-confidence and Optimism 39

Chapter 5   Go Big: Drive and Determination 53

Chapter 6   Go Big: Intellect, Intent, and Implementation ... 63

Chapter 7   Go Big: Values and Vision 74

Chapter 8   Go Big: Time Management 90

Chapter 9   Go Big: Environment and Exposure 100

Chapter 10 Go Big: Enthusiasm and Epiphanies 115

Chapter 11 Go Big: Creativity and Charisma 127

Chapter 12 Go Big: Patience and Persistence 144

Chapter 13 Go Big: Processing Change 154

Chapter 14 Go Big: Defined by Discipline 167

Chapter 15 Go Big: Mentors Matter 175

Conclusion 183

Bibliography 187

Acknowledgments

Every written expression I share entails an epiphany from heaven. Incredibly, this writing gift from God takes me places I can only imagine. Yet, ultimately, to God be all the glory for the things He has done.

Unashamedly, I am a saved, transformed, maturing Christian. For nearly fifty years, I have lived a converted, born-again, and radically altered life through the sacrificial work of the risen Christ. Daily I live by His power, pray in His name, and process life through the prism of His love. In all things, I seek to walk in obedience to His kingdom principles while sharing Him with others.

In prayerful meditation and all throughout each day, there is a still small voice guiding my steps. It represents the indwelling presence of God's Holy Spirit. When I reach the limits of my conceptual capacities while writing, in just the right manner and moment God's Spirit leads me to the exact book, article, historical quote, allusion, anecdote, or conversation that opens the floodgates of literary flow.

From the human plane, I bless the Lord for our church family. Without the saints of the Pleasant Green Baptist Church in Kansas City, Kansas, my life has little meaning. With more than sixteen years of service here, I am still enjoying the honeymoon! They are an incredible people, exercising phenomenal faith in God and in me, despite my severe limitations.

I offer genuine gratitude to my church staff: Sis. Mamie Keith—a model of efficiency, dependability, indefatigability; Sis. Sheila Williams—gifted in prayer, ever-faithful, supportive, dedicated. Also, we have tremendous assets by way of volunteers who help us reach the world for Christ! Let's keep advancing the kingdom of God with these books.

No book that bears my name exists without my solid research team, the Office of the Pastor. Again, you did the bulk of this—starting with the concept, to tracking down sources, to transcribing audio files, through offering marketing suggestions. These steps nurture the writing process. Bless you for one more book!

Each written endeavor is touched by the prayerfulness, wisdom, careful eyes, suggestions, and high grammatical standards of Sis. Helen Gray, my "in-house" editor. You did it again!

The publishing family of Townsend Press of the Sunday School Publishing Board, led by Dr. Derrick Jackson, are appreciatively applauded. Special commendation to the designers, editors, sales team, marketers, and staff in Nashville for enhancing this work. Special gratitude is extended to Rev. Debra Berry for all her help!

So many long time friends and beloved colleagues will hear their thoughts (often without attribution!) in this book. Unwittingly, they have shared gems with me in countless conversations. This book is deeper, richer, and better because you allowed me to interrogate you as my initial audience for several ideas. What a focus group. I truly thank you, one and all.

I sincerely appreciate my family: my brilliant wife, Jennifer, and two fine children, Jarvis II and Jillian. Bless the Master for all my "Js." Thank you for enriching me!

My beloved mother, Mrs. Ellen R. Jones, went home to be with the Master before this book reached publication. Every day since her departure in January 2015 I have missed her wisdom, smile, counsel, laughter, and ability to offer just what I needed to "go big" as a Christian, minister, pastor, author, denominational leader, speaker, prophetic activist, and stalwart in the Christian faith. Momma, I really miss your smile, your love, your determination, your toughness, and your peach cobbler!

My siblings Bruce, Janice, and Reginald have allowed me to soar! I am blessed by them as we grow in the wisdom of God, our mother's faith, and our family experiences. They read my books and offer helpful commentary.

Introduction

Over the last few years, most have heard some variation on the interesting advertising tagline, "Go big or go home!" In various contexts, it has reached a cultural saturation point. Upon examination, it represents a cute phrase inspired by Madison Avenue media. It conveys aiming for unusual success with a number of important components—integrity, creativity, fervency, vigor, exposure, and mentoring, blended with drive and determination. After repeatedly hearing that phrase, however, I felt compelled to scrutinize it for insight and practical application for everyday living.

With prayerful reflection, I discerned that this pithy truth aptly captures a powerful life philosophy. When its insights are fully examined and its principles applied, it leads to tremendous breakthroughs as millions assess, adapt, and aim toward next-level achievements. So I thought that grappling with the meaning of "go big or go home" might help us transition from excitement and hype to "Now, what must I do?" The latter, harder task transforms great slogans into dynamic personal agendas.

Each person on earth has been allotted 24 hours each day, 7 days a week, and 365 days spread over 52 weeks or 12 months, comprising one year. No one has more minutes, hours, days, or weeks than another. So, then, something more than time must account for why some achieve while others languish in excuses, defeat, and mediocrity. One distinguishing characteristic between individuals must be the degree to which some embrace the "go big" notion while others are satisfied with the "go home" default mechanism.

As my primary objective involves fostering a cadre of "go big" thinkers, I will very briefly touch upon sad contours of the "go home" lifestyle. Descriptions of the latter should serve to heighten deliberation upon the former.

I write to inspire younger persons scanning the windshield, moving into a world of relationships, careers, and dreams. Also, I write to older persons who may erroneously believe that their best days are in the rearview window. No! Rather, "go big" thinkers come in all ages, cultures, classes, ethnicities, and locales, and from humble origins.

The body of this work shall comprise thorough examination of the confluence of qualities that lead to exceptional attainment: self-confidence, optimism, drive, desire, integrity, determination, intellect, intent, values, vision, environment, exposure, epiphanies, hard work, creativity, persistence, energy, timing, enthusiasm, creativity, wit, charisma, patience, persistence, radical self-assessment, mentors, and more. As I hope you will discern, such analysis brings infinite joy to my heart.

In every case, while there are latent tendencies within all persons, there must be deliberate attempts to sharpen these qualities. After evaluating them, I will offer suggestions on honing critical skills in order to achieve the "go big" dream.

Indeed, I am fascinated by those who scale heights of prominence in various disciplines: literature, philosophy, theology, medicine, science, engineering, sports, journalism, fine arts, politics, academia, medicine, law, architecture, psychology, economics, sociology, information technology, social networking, and more.

This book shall reveal many exciting principles for success, adopting the "go big" mindset. It shall also lead to life-transforming adventures designed to enhance faith in God, strategic thinking, education, relationships, careers, family life, and self-image while helping all cope with inevitable hindrances to progress.

If this book proves successful, it shall enliven a dormant spirit in you and ignite a spark of creativity. You will move from merely admiring the triumphs of others to the place where you become an achiever, an overcomer, a success, and a "discussed" person in your own right. Entertainers, athletes, and politicians are not the only people "marked out" for attainment. You can be an unusual success if you deign to "go big." It's available to you!

More than merely reading another interesting book, I propose that you use this one as a practical goad toward your success!

Now, let's get to work!

Chapter 1

The "Go Big" Way

By nature, I am analytical in my thinking. Intuitively, I deconstruct concepts, notions, and ideas, never accepting any assertion at face value. Something deep and visceral in me finds fault with "conventional wisdom." I yearn for empirical evidence from impeccable sources before I accept assertions as meaningful truth. While I highly respect esteemed authorities, only God's revelation—the Bible—escapes my bracing, harsh, and full critique!

While reading a wide variety of media (novels, newspapers, periodicals, professional journals, blogs, and social media sources), I maintain a critical eye, aiming to see more than is apparent from a cursory reading. Mere existence in print does not validate such as an authoritative source.

Further, maturity has taught me to be skeptical of surface appraisals, for I have found them to be incomplete and inconclusive. So when I hear the mantra "Go big!" I must thoroughly investigate its meaning (nuance, components).

Fundamentally, I seek wisdom from God along with insight and depth. For too long, in my view, many have accepted glib formulations without deconstructing the assertions.

I seek to conceptualize beyond the "cute" factor of the "go big" phrase. I desire to ascertain how it might alter my thoughts while transforming my behavior. If it is true, it will give me a prism for viewing subsequent reality. If it proves false, I cast it aside as fatally flawed. Fundamentally, I hold that individuals choose their paths through the grace of God.

Over time, I believe that God has prevented me from making serious errors because I have trusted Him to give me spiritual discernment. As my mother might say, "All that glitters is not gold." Similarly, this "go big" idea must be scrutinized.

Therefore, let us examine the undergirding philosophy of "go big":

"Go big" exercises absolute reverence for God, respect for others, as well as self-confidence, intelligence, experience, exposure, freedom, imagination, enthusiasm, and many other positive traits.

"Go big" projects a sublime, noble, and high expectation indicative of zeal, fortitude, resilience, and unrelenting dedication.

"Go big" articulates fresh, ahead-of-their-times, prophetic, radical, near-revolutionary concepts. Indeed, these might represent to some rather strange notions.

"Go big" expects outstanding achievement irrespective of others' opinions, delays, detours, or temporary setbacks. Once on that road, you can never deviate from it. You are propelled by its intrigue. You must explore it fully!

"Go big" expresses the trajectory of your ambition, signaling something momentous, meaningful, and majestic—far from the mundane.

"Go big" radiates a positive, assured, poised vibe, warning others of the intent to make a discernable difference in the world.

"Go big" resonates within you, refusing to be comfortable around resentment, envy, jealousy, gossip, negativity, or ignorance. Those engulfed by buffoonery, pettiness, wasted opportunities, shortcuts, gimmicks, or the "easy way" will never succeed!

Overtaken by "go big," you respond to the invisible, hear the inaudible, and expect the incredible, all while living by the intangible. In summation, it's inexpressible!

"Go big" signals that if God needs a vessel through whom He chooses to work, you eagerly volunteer for His assignment. Its fulfillment, then, becomes your life's mission.

"Go big" asks four questions: 1) If not me, then who? 2) If not this, then what? 3) If not now, then when? 4) If not here, then where? Self-commissioned, you immediately engage!

"Go big" draws attention to unconventional thinking, creativity, courage, veering from the beaten path, asking probing questions, leaving others to traffic in conventional modes of operation. Now, you understand why you are different from others.

"Go big" shatters feeble expectations, as you would rather lead than idly watch the parade of humanity as it marches toward substantive achievement.

"Go big" clarifies the need for bold, ambitious, audacious, aggressive initiatives, claiming new territory rather than being satisfied with land already possessed. Endowed with this spirit, you want and need more, to fulfill a higher purpose.

"Go big" intentionally writes a legacy of significant engagement while alive without leaving it to others for possible misrepresentation, misinterpretation, or omission after your death.

"Go big" develops its own lexicon: large, enormous, stupendous, consequential, unprecedented, amazing, phenomenal, mind-blowing, monumental, spectacular, miraculous, sustained; and then it employs such notions in normative daily conversation and expectation.

"Go big" involves unusual objectives, defying doubt (both internal and external) while venturing forth into the vortex of uncertainty and danger.

"Go big" seizes the moment, scales the heights, expecting divine and human favor along a wonderful journey of self-discovery.

Because of your "go big" attitude, you refuse to accept average, mediocre, regular, or "whatever," as you know something infinitely better lies just over the horizon.

"Go big" aligns itself with like-minded thinkers, producing a synergy of efforts. Gradually, you begin to relish the company of other achievers.

As you are driven by some internal mechanism, "go big" sees your mirror reflection of a supra-achiever, an overcomer, a champion, or a victor despite temporary challenges, hindrances, setbacks, and deferrals.

"Go big" quotes Scripture, reads widely, recalls wise aphorisms, remembers important anecdotes, sees historical parallels, and verifies sources of information/insight all as a means of encouraging oneself.

"Go big" casts aside failures of yesterday, knowing that today and tomorrow are unknown gifts from God.

"Go big" deliberately pivots toward the next step, acutely aware of each previous misstep, receiving forgiveness, walking in grace, and trusting God throughout the process.

While ruminating on this "go big" notion, I was struck by a fascinating book by Mark Batterson, entitled *All In*. In it, he captures the essence of my thinking: "You are only one decision away from a totally different life. Of course, it will probably be the toughest decision you'll ever make. But if you have the courage to completely surrender yourself to the lordship of Jesus Christ, there is no telling what God will do. All bets are off because all bets are on God."

"Go big" properly interprets all events, disavowing highs or lows as definitive of life's full picture.

"Go big" continually reinvents itself, integrating new information, new technology, new challenges, emerging trends, God's manifestation, and the zeitgeist, as change represents life's only constant.

"Go big" celebrates an iconic American and international hall of fame: George Washington, Thomas Jefferson, Benjamin Franklin, Alexander Hamilton, Phillis Wheatley, Abraham Lincoln, Sojourner Truth, Harriett Tubman, Frederick Douglass, Booker T. Washington, George Washington Carver, Albert Einstein, W. E. B. DuBois, Franklin D. Roosevelt, Ralph Bunche, Pablo Picasso, Ernest Hemingway, Wolfgang Mozart, Johann Bach, Ludwig van Beethoven, Frederic Chopin, Jonas Salk, Sigmund Freud, Marie Curie, Martin Luther King Jr., Malcolm X, Charles Drew, Bill Gates, Steve Jobs, Mark Zuckerberg, and legions of other achievers.

This fraternity of the successful was connected by an innate sense that life for them and for others could be better. That better life, however, absolutely required their full engagement—mind, heart, words, and actions.

"Go big" changes the paradigm, flips the script, reorients the direction, telling of an unseen future, a different vision, as others are beguiled and stupefied by its sheer audacity.

"Go big" laughs at obstacles, winks at trouble, and transcends adversity while being carried along by faith in God, never giving in, giving out, or giving up.

"Go big" represents a long-term soliloquy toward uncommon attainment, even as there is little to show for your declaration. Yet inwardly, you remain fixated on the unfailing ideology, idea, and ideal that failure is not a viable option.

"Go big" depicts that you are ill-suited for mundane living, tired of "just enough," unable to successfully operate under the radar, nauseated by the meager, and always affirming God's next manifestation.

At this point, you may need to put down this book because all of it is designed to explode your sense of satisfaction, no matter your present level of attainment.

This warning is given early because if you continue reading, something will happen in the cognitive circuitry of your cerebral cortex. Indeed, with new information your brain will react in ways that challenge you to embrace the electricity and explosive content inherent in going big.

"Go big" celebrates successive rungs on the ladder of engagement, oblivious to the possibility of a final summit. One mountain scaled prepares you for another!

"Go big" represents dissatisfaction with the stale, traditional, trivial, trite, irrelevant view, affirming the necessity for creativity, innovation, and unique thinking for sustained progress.

"Go big" signals the inherent danger in playing it safe, taking the low road, fearing critics, risking nothing, while just hoping for different results.

"Go big" refuses to ask anyone's permission to attempt grand objectives; rather, it profoundly and boldly takes the initiative. As others discuss it, you go ahead and get it done!

As you continue reading, I pray for the aha! moment, as you realize that in describing this "go big" personality, I am really describing you!

"Go big" risks doubt, derision, and ridicule for stupendous undertakings while ignoring accolades in the aftermath of success. Whether others acknowledge you or not, you know that "go big" represents unusual attainment.

"Go big" constantly raises the standard of biblical, spiritual, moral, and personal excellence from the perspective of Christ, ensuring that any achievement aligns with a decidedly theocentric worldview.

"Go big" maintains its march wisely, steadily, and resolutely, fighting doubts within and disputes without.

"Go big" finds infinite joy in a limitless, expansive, grand room—the spacious one called "room for improvement."

"Go big" rejects average counsel: "Wait for a better season; wait for a better venue; wait for a better objective; wait for better revenue; wait for better allies."

Instead, knowing the brevity of life, "go big" asks, "Why wait? What's wrong with doing it now?" If you do it now and fail, you still have time to try again, differently.

"Go big" in baseball swings for the homerun rather than accepting singles and doubles, though they too are valuable in scoring.

"Go big" in golf charges the greens, shoots for the hole, sinks the hard putt, and claims the low score while negating thoughts of choking or failing.

"Go big" in basketball clears out the defense, demands the last shot, waits until the last second, and heaves the ball, accepting credit for the victory or blame for the defeat. That's why sports enthusiasts celebrate LeBron James, Kobe Bryant, Stephen Curry, James Harden, and Kevin Durant. In your thoughts, you should join that company!

"Go big" in motorsports exceeds the track's speed record, takes the hairpin turn, bumps another vehicle, and forsakes caution lights, anticipating the checkered flag at the end. In that regard, Kurt Busch, Dale Earnhardt Jr., Chase Elliott, Jeff Gordon, Kevin Harvick, Jimmie Johnson, Kasey Kahne, and others deserve special recognition.

"Go big" in boxing accepts height/weight/reach variances, bloodied face, fatigue, and raw emotion, expecting to land the right blow at the right moment, felling the opponent while taking home the championship belt. Famous names emerge in those discussions: Max Schmeling, Rocky Marciano, Joe Louis, Muhammad Ali, "Sugar" Ray Leonard, Mike Tyson (pre-rape conviction), Larry Holmes, Evander Holyfield, Thomas "Hitman" Hearns, and Floyd Mayweather.

"Go big" with indifference to naysayers. Having launched a news network that competes with CBS, NBC, and ABC and provides live news with a global reach, thirty-plus years later CNN yet sustains itself as the "world news leader."

"Go big" depicts the mayor of Charleston, South Carolina, telling his staff that no matter the consequences, the Confederate flag (symbolic of entrenched defiance, rebellion, treason, and segregation in the South) must come down! And despite determined opposition, it did!

"Go big" captured Franklin Delano Roosevelt, crippled by polio, yet assuring a frightened nation, "The only thing we have to fear is fear itself." His words buoyed American hopes while saving the Western world from Nazi tyranny.

"Go big" aligns with Teddy Roosevelt's dictum to would-be achievers: "Go into the arena." Yet, the road to attainment is fraught with danger.

"Go big" echoes Ronald Reagan telling the Soviets, "Mr. Gorbachev, tear down this wall." That clarion call signaled an end to Communist dominance in Eastern Europe while serving as the death blow to atheistic socialism globally.

"Go big" marks Dr. Martin Luther King Jr.'s challenging the fundamentals of American ideals: "Let freedom ring!"

"Go big" prompts a craze most didn't know they needed—social networking—then enrolls millions, empowering Facebook, Instagram, Pinterest, YouTube, Twitter, and more to revolutionize the varied ways humans interact.

"Go big" encourages medical research, unleashing new treatments, new protocols, and new methods, vastly extending the frontiers of science. Virulent diseases have been eradicated from earth because some scientist kept probing possibilities.

While such names and moments are well known, the world awaits your "go big" contribution. Remember this: there is still time remaining to etch your accomplishments on the wall of human attainment.

"Go big" motivates your aspiration to greatness, prompting you to strive toward your full capacity for virtue and dedication to uncommon objectives.

"Go big" marks a seemingly obsessive proclivity, a driving force, a consuming passion, a relentless undertaking, separating achievers from others.

"Go big," during the American civil rights struggle, forced bigoted, hate-filled racists to relent; it waged a moral war without tanks, aircraft, guns, ammunition, or armor; it utilized principles of nonviolent resistance with regular, determined footsoldiers marching and singing, "Ain't Gonna Let Nobody Turn Me 'Round."

"Go big," despite determined opposition in Congress, counts among its victories the Civil Rights Act, the Voting Rights Act, public accommodations provisions, a changed America, and more, hastening guaranteed yet unfilled freedoms for people dogged by four hundred years of injustice, all due to dark pigmentation of their skin.

Amid centuries of racism (overt, systemic, and personal), segregation, hostility, and injustice, "Go big" characterizes a dignified generation of African-American leaders: statesmen, judges, journalists, entertainers, corporate executives, school administrators, medical professionals, attorneys, authors, mayors, activists, ministers, workers, homemakers and others, knocking on closed doors.

Until finally in 2008, "Go big" spawns the ultimate political, psychological, and social transformation: the election of America's first black president!

Despite obvious advances in racial relations, "Go big" does not accept present-day America, however, as post-racial.

I sincerely pray to God that more people (you!) will embrace this captivating, inspiring, compelling, world-changing ideal inherent in the notion of "go big."

Some time ago, a dear friend encouraged me to purchase a copy of a riveting book by Malcolm Gladwell entitled *David and Goliath*. Although this book examines the biblical story of history's greatest military mismatch, it is not religious in nature, tone, or focus. Rather, through a secular analysis Gladwell aims to explore "underdogs, misfits, and the art of battling giants." God intervenes and works through us to defeat literal, personal, emotional, psychological, relational, and spiritual giants standing before us. In reading Gladwell's insights, I discovered the perfect segue for exploration of the larger "go big" concept.

In the Bible, 1 Samuel 16–17 offers four sweeping principles for living the "go big" life:

1) Character–Internal Evaluation by God

These two chapters cited in Holy Writ reveal a gracious God willing to use a man beyond his family's (and, perhaps, his own) perception. Last of the eight sons of Jesse, David is left out in the field as the prophet comes to anoint (oil poured on the head of) one son as the next king of Israel.

Absent God's analysis of him, David would remain a mere footnote in the divine-human drama. Yet, in the plan of God he demonstrates unusual character: loyal son, gifted musician, mighty man of valor, a warrior, prudent in speech, charismatic, and endowed with favor from the Lord (anointed)

Everyone may not do great exploits, but everyone can strive for good character. Indeed, "God sees not as man sees, for man looks at the outward appearance, but the LORD looks at the heart" (1 Samuel 16:7b). What God saw in the character of David set him apart from others in his family, others in that area, others in that era, and others throughout recorded history.

"Character" references the best analysis of an individual. Another description of character references the aggregate of features and traits that form the individual's nature. God, Christ, the Holy Spirit, tested friends, family members, close observers, and the spiritually mature are best able to discern character.

In every important endeavor, you must pray to God for revelation of the character of those with whom you may interact (husband, wife, business partner, and others). Many hurts and calamities can be avoided if you ask God to show you the ugly, unreliable, duplicitous, hypocritical, judgmental, mean, bitter, cynical character of others. And in the process, He may show your character to you! Above every other distinctive trait, "Go big" people exemplify good character, though not perfection!

In the sight of God, availability trumps mere ability. In His hands, we achieve beyond our wildest estimation: "Now to Him who is able to do far more abundantly beyond all that we ask or think, according to the power that works within us" (Ephesians 3:20).

In short, well before they actually "arrive," the character of "go big" people illustrates they are destined for more than ordinary exploits!

2) Curiosity–Truly Understand What's at Stake

Still in the two chapters noted above, 1 Samuel 16–17, we see the intriguing, riveting drama of this warfare. Early on, David is curious as to the nature of the engagement, the combatants, and the reward for the victor while questioning his role in it. Hear David's pertinent question: "For who is this uncircumcised Philistine, that he should taunt the armies of the living God?" (1 Samuel 17:26c).

Goliath, in David's view, is more than a bad bully, mammoth miscreant, or a large irritant; instead, he is an objectionable obstacle to the worship of the Almighty God. Goliath interferes with David's and the Israelites' object of worship. Thus, the giant must inevitably fall!

Curiosity never ceases to investigate, to explore, to ask impertinent questions, to probe, and to wonder. Indeed, many find these aspects of curiosity offensive, for often they defy the accepted version of what is allowable. Yet, if you are to succeed you must possess curiosity.

My mentors were persons who pushed the envelope, asking questions that challenged my thinking. I am forever grateful to God and to them for pushing me out of my comfort zone.

The "go big" mentality surveys the situation at hand and then, when necessary, accepts personal responsibility for action as others demur, debate, conjure excuses, wallow in self-pity, relent, or fall prey to doubts. Not surprisingly, "go big" thinkers graduate from universities, found companies, write screenplays, find cures for stubborn diseases, publish poetry, establish foundations, and in the process, transform the world! Often, it all starts in curiosity: "Why not?"

Curiosity fuels engagement because substantive change requires you to ask questions deeper than others consider safe or acceptable. As a potential achiever, you should never fear challenging the status quo!

Life remains boring and stale if you simply awaken, get out of bed, prepare for the day, turn the pages of the datebook or calendar, and move in the familiar. Instead, you should look in the mirror while asking, "Today, what can change for me, and for my world?"

3) Courage–Risking More than Others

Further, here in 1 Samuel 16–17, David teaches the importance of staring fear in the face and using available instruments (sling and stones). While they are crude tools in comparison to the giant's massive size, shield, and sword, in the hand of an anointed shepherd-boy on a divine mission they will prove quite formidable. Indeed, going against Goliath might be viewed by some as suicidal, while, by God's evaluation, it typifies courage of the first magnitude.

David frames his intention as an act of bravery, courage, and determination: "Let no man's heart fail on account of [Goliath]; your servant will go and fight with this Philistine" (1 Samuel 17:32). Clearly, David recognizes Goliath's greater size, superior skills, and extensive war experience; yet, David will fight him. As most evaluate Goliath as too big to fight, David views him as too big to miss with godly weaponry. Now, that's world-changing courage!

Throughout this biblical narrative, we note David's concern for protecting the integrity of God as Goliath's life epitomizes a real and credible threat to the existence of God's people. So David approaches him in the might given by God. In short, for David this battle represents an encounter in the supernatural realm. Aided by the Almighty, David's courage will commence, continue, and culminate the conflict.

Contemporary giants (guilt, futility, unemployment, poverty, dropout, drugs, incarceration, family dysfunction, income inequality, and domestic abuse) will fall, provided those of the "go big" persuasion step forward to chart a path toward victory. You have a choice: tell your sad story of neglect, abuse, mistreatment, or whatever. Or use your story (everyone has one) to propel you toward the best inside of you. Often, leaders are not elected or appointed; instead, they lead by extraordinary example. And when you do so, people will follow.

The 2016 Republican presidential campaign started with fifteen or more candidates (governors, senators, business executives, and more). Over time, the field was whittled, with surprising outcomes. Indeed, fearmongering, boldness, pandering, and cunning characterized the eventual Republican nominee.

Further, movies inspire millions as they tap into emotions we all feel, even when we don't always act on them. *Mr. Smith Goes to Washington* depicts the courage of a young, idealistic senator (Jimmy Stewart) facing a corrupt Washington political culture. Despite considerable odds and estimable obstacles, Smith prevails over entrenched "giants" in the United States Senate. Rereleased on DVD sixty years after its premiere, millions relive the vicarious joy of viewing courage in action. Despite simplistic sentimentality, that film expresses "go big" in action.

4) Commitment–Work to Complete the Task

In explaining the basis for confidence in defeating Goliath, David recounts past experiences: "The LORD who delivered me from the paw of the lion and from the paw of the bear, He will deliver me from the hand of this Philistine" (1 Samuel 17:37). In two ways, with two animals, David recalls dynamic divine encounters.

In David's words, two ideas should capture our attention: 1) David feels utter repugnance regarding Goliath, calling him not by name, but "this uncircumcised Philistine"; and, 2) David acknowledges the Lord of the past (subduing ferocious, feared animals) who works in the present (defeating giants). If God did it before, David reasons, He can do it again!

The "go big" sentiment captures those who, like David, will not yield in commitment to divinely ordained tasks. Instead, he sees them through to the very end, no matter what. Commitment works harder and longer, enduring more, risking more, hurting more, as it celebrates in the end! Are you in that category?

In our day, we celebrate instant success rather than those who should earn our respect by their commitment. Scores of secular artists (rock, blues, soul, pop, or rap) today, for example, are one-hit wonders over against those who have compiled impressive discographies over a thirty- or forty-year career.

In my view, deep commitment still leads to significant achievement. Monuments in our nation's capital are there because individuals displayed the highest measure of commitment to American ideals: freedom, democracy, patriotism, valor, courage, sacrifice, and more.

Finally, David receives special recognition as Israel's esteemed king, with a distinguished lineage leading all the way to the Messiah, the Redeemer, our Savior, Jesus Christ. Notwithstanding obvious moral failures and ethical transgressions, David bears the biblical imprimatur "a man after God's own heart" (see Acts 13:22). Part of that reckoning must be based on his "go big" vision for the things of God. Indeed, "go big" people feel divinely ordained for unusual achievements. They live by divine destiny, infused with an enduring sense of life purpose.

In the New Testament, "go big" identifies a gracious God dispatching His only Son, Jesus Christ, to foster human reconciliation, ultimately sending that Son to an old, despised, and rugged cross, the Roman emblem of suffering, ignominy, and shame.

Incredibly, "go big" captures the inability of the grave to hold the Son of God, for early that Sunday morning, God robbed death of its sting while simultaneously taking victory from the grave.

Marvelously, "go big" describes the glorious plan of salvation: Christ atones for the sin of humanity by His innocence, accepting what He did not owe (sin debt) while giving humanity what it did not deserve (imputed righteousness).

In consideration of the "go big" mentality, many may remain unconvinced of its limitless impact, as so few express similar conceptualization. Sadly, you might disavow such a spirit, feeling your life to be inconsequential, ordinary, and blasé. To you, I offer words of infinite hope: Nothing changes in you, for you, and through you until you change your mind.

The human mind has limitless power and potential. Remember the children's story of *The Little Engine that Could:* "I think I can, I think I can, I think I can." This new thought or renewed process captures the key to your internal transformation.

Chapter 2

Sad Tales of "Go Home"

Only due to the necessity of a balanced presentation shall I attempt to express what characterizes those who choose the "go home" philosophy. These observations stem from reviewing life choices of so many who could have taken a different route.

For so many, now that you are on a particular path, it seems impossible to change your course. Perhaps things just didn't turn out right! Incredibly, you may reason, "It's too late for me." "If only I had read this book ten or twenty years earlier, maybe things would have been different." Or, "If I hadn't made that move, I could be further along." No matter your perspective, as long as you are alive, God gives you unlimited hope and unlimited opportunities.

In fact, this book is designed especially for those who went home (pun intended) and couldn't live in simple "houses"—walls of woe, décor of defeat, furniture of failure, carpet of compromise, and appliances of agony. So instead, they changed addresses. They de-camped, deciding to "go big." I celebrate that fateful choice!

Truly, life pivots on whether you choose to "go big" or "go home." Please remember the previous chapter as you compare it with the present one.

Variously stated, "go home" captures bitterness, resentment, fault finding, acquiescence, fatalism, and apathy. Indeed, you might embrace anything other than personal responsibility for your place in the world.

"Go home" people married too soon, had children before seeing all options, didn't remain in college, never left American soil, never met other ethnicities, and now have limited exposure.

"Go home" people operate in fear: What might happen if I try? They enjoy the familiar comfort of a few friends and well-known associates. They ridicule new adventures, new options, and new planning.

"Go home" thoughts exist in long-ago achievements, faded plaques, browned certificates, and moments of rapture now dwarfed by present realities.

"Go home" resigns itself to defeat, unflattering character flaws, negative self-appraisals, excuse making, fluctuating emotions, and ugly cynicism mired in a "woe is me" attitude.

"Go home," without uttering the words, surmises, "I've been knocked down; why should I aim to get up?" And thus, the defeatist mentality keeps you down!

"Go home" emerges from the crucible of job loss, bitter divorce, increasing debt, teen parentage, sexual abuse, being widowed, facing eviction, repossession, tax problems, physical illness, family grief, serious reversals, or any adversity.

"Go home" longs for the company of the complacent, having sent out engraved invitations to a special pity-party. They resign themselves to the proposition, "I am the only one to have suffered like this."

"Go home" remembers and, incredibly, often relishes every rejection, every mean person, every slight, every roadblock, and every closed door, allowing others to determine your success or failure.

"Go home" basks in victimhood, wallowing in self-pity, reliving the entire trauma, making them definitive for a life of low achievement: "If not for X, I could have succeeded."

"Go home" rushes to the easy explanation of racism, even as it does exist in America and the world, but it is not the root of all situations.

"Go home" operates amid "would'a, could'a, should'a," remaining nostalgic about warm, cozy moments that will never return.

"Go home" aligns with the ignorant, the belligerent, the uncouth, the lazy, the immoral, and the silly—those comfortable within the parameters of the possible.

"Go home" is keen to angst and attracted to drama, giving undue attention to slights, disagreements, confrontations, negativity, attitudes, gossip, and rumors, failing to dismiss such as part of the productivity package leading to sustained advancement.

"Go home" illustrates a proclivity toward lethargy and lassitude, exhausted by early energy expenditures so that, now, enthusiasm is depleted.

"Go home" capitulates to external forces, finding relief in small vistas, narrow agendas, negligible progress, and simple strategies, being satisfied to just survive for another day.

"Go home" expresses unwillingness to explore the new, the intriguing, the mysterious, the uncertain, and the adventurous, sensing that such requires too much exertion—physical, intellectual, and volitional—without guaranteeing a positive outcome.

"Go home" bows, scrapes, hangs its head, slumps its shoulders, gives up, gives in, and gives out. Often, just then you may be on the threshold of an incredible, God-ordained victory of epic proportions!

"Go home" never attempts so as to never fail, operating in the shadows, under the radar, fearful of advancement, and languishing in the average.

"Go home" evidences itself in extreme risk aversion, afraid even to attempt the unusual and afraid to succeed, resulting in a perpetual condition of dissatisfaction.

As I reflect on this "go home" syndrome, I am reminded of a turning point in my life, without which this book would not have existed. Let me tell you about it.

I graduated from an urban, tough, gritty high school in 1977. I was, however, near the top of my class. I applied and was admitted to at least seven major universities, including Stanford and USC. Because of tight finances, I opted for the University of California, Berkeley, which provided ample financial aid, grants, and more. (Thank God, no student loans!)

Once there, my English tests determined that I needed a remedial writing course. A kind professor patiently showed me how to properly integrate grammatical marks in my writing. He encouraged me at a time of emotional challenge.

Today, I reflect on the fact that that professor had the power to wreck my dream of written expression. Indeed, negative words could have prompted a defeatist "go home" trajectory, perhaps dropping my studies and forsaking a degree path. Instead, I graduated with a bachelor's degree in four years with confidence that I had some latent talents in writing.

Now, in the process of completing my tenth book, I believe by the grace of God I can safely say I have something to say and the gifts to say it thoughtfully, boldly, and clearly.

Get the moral of that short story: Don't let anybody cause you to "go home"!

"Go home," in hindsight, recalls itself as just as educated, just as talented as achievers, or even more so, but luck ran out, and the "ship didn't come in." Remember, you are much better than that supposition. Rather than waiting for your "ship" to come in, go out and meet it on the ocean of creativity!

"Go home" represents blissful mediocrity comforted by small victories while leisurely strolling lanes of futility.

"Go home" continually operates in fear rather than faith, imagining every negative scenario in the way of your success, stalling every positive step.

A word of self-disclosure: after nearly forty years of Christian ministry, primarily preaching the Gospel of Jesus Christ before audiences large and small, I still experience the fear of nervous anticipation. Incredibly, God always works in the preaching moment, bringing glory to His name. I simply need to stand up in order that God will show up in me.

"Go home" depicts abject failure, returning to a warm, inviting place dressed in the garb of a loser! You are not characterized as such until you actually accept it.

After such a dismal chronicle of the ways the "go home" spirit diminishes the human character, I must add that there are no known statesmen, economists, renown thinkers, judges, journalists, educators, artists, musicians, inventors, entrepreneurs, activists, scientists, or change agents in this cohort.

Search as I might, no data exist, no books written, no plays performed, no movies filmed, no businesses begun, no songs recorded, no place in history reserved, no outstanding achievements are known for those who took the easy way, joining the millions of anonymous faces who chose to "go home" in misery.

In a riveting narrative from the Old Testament, God instructs Moses to send twelve spies (one from each of Israel's tribes) to reconnoiter the Promised Land. In Numbers 13–14, we note the contrast between those possessed of the "go big" mentality versus those of the "go home" variety, and the results of that difference.

"Go big" comprises two men of faith: Joshua and Caleb. On the other hand, "go home" includes far more men—ten to be exact. Their names are left in the dustbin of history. Without an open Bible, I challenge anyone to recount the names of the ten spies in the "go home" category. And that is as it should be; none would become men of renown because they failed to honor God! Whenever would-be achievers "go home," the world never remembers them!

The scenario of Numbers 14:4 sags with sadness, pathos, and poignancy: "So they said to one another, 'Let us appoint a leader and return to Egypt.'" Arguably, this verse represents history's greatest capitulation to tough odds, underscoring the ultimate "go home" sensibility.

After all Israel had gone through (Egyptian oppression through heavy-handed work conditions, lack of freedom, and denial to worship God and more), its decision to return to Egypt after a taste of liberty along with struggles in the wilderness served as a veritable insult to God. It is good that "the glory of the LORD appeared in the tent of meeting to all the sons of Israel" (Numbers 14:10). This dynamic manifestation reaffirming the will of God vetoed Israel's plans to return to Egyptian bondage.

Moreover, closer to Christian reality in the glorious plan of God, the Word of God proves that the "go home" perspective is difficult to maintain because of the Son of God, Jesus Christ. Once saved by Christ, God fosters in His disciples (you and me) a yearning to strive for more, pray for more, work for more, seek more, sacrifice more, sow more, invest more, and endure more, constantly reminding us of God's inexhaustible "more" for His children.

A searing truth that brings this "go home" matter from concept to concrete reality occurred in the life of a friend thirty years ago. In the early 1990s, a friend stated that her college tuition was quite high. Her father had run out of financial resources to pay the bill. He called her to commiserate, suggesting she drop out of school, at best delaying, or at worst ending her dream of academic success. In fact, he had already borrowed a truck to haul her possessions home!

Worried but determined, she prayed to God for wisdom. She decided that, somehow, she would remain in college. In fact, she disregarded her conversation with her father. She resolved not to "go home."

She reasoned that literally to go home would mean 1) disappointing family, friends, and supporters; 2) suffering humiliation from high school alumni; 3) defeat in a worthy endeavor; 4) allowing finances (or the lack thereof) to dictate the acquisition of a quality education; 5) the end of meaningful academic pursuits; 6) death to professional objectives; and, 7) the beginning of a downward spiral in life.

The good news is, through scholarships, federal Pell grants, and work-study, she paid her tuition, continued her education, and graduated from that prestigious university before going on to professional acclaim.

Indeed, life has several crucial turning points. They present opportunities for persons to opt out of taking the literal or figurative "go home" route. When viewed in hindsight, you may hardly fathom God's remarkable interventions combined with your willingness to work hard, work creatively, and work long-term.

At the same time, I recall a relative whom my mother earnestly tried to pry away from her small-town existence, with its narrow vistas in Louisiana. So my mother invited her niece to Los Angeles, California, for its greater opportunities. Excitedly, we discussed all that she might see and do under the protective care of her new family in the big city. Sadly, she refused to venture forth, hopelessly in love with her high school sweetheart.

We can only imagine what her life would have been, the bounty of options available to her if she had had the courage to leave home in the first place. (In this sense, staying home was tantamount to the "go home" attitude.) In either case, one may live a life of "What if?"

Truly, I celebrate the legions of those who refused the advice of the well-meaning to "go home."

Isabel Wilkerson, in her widely well-received book *The Warmth of Other Suns: The Epic Story of America's Great Migration*, recounts several searing narratives of determined black people who left their native home in the American South in search of greater opportunities (educational, personal, and professional) in other parts of America. They represent the ultimate "go big" thinkers.

In new lands under the warmth of other suns in Chicago, Milwaukee, Cleveland, New York, Philadelphia, Denver, San Francisco, Los Angeles, and other places, these black pioneers became physicians, engineers, attorneys, judges, homemakers, civic leaders, change agents, ministers, and business leaders in their new hometowns across America. Could you similarly imagine such an audacious journey? Now, how about envisioning such for yourself?

Wilkerson chronicles their struggles under "other suns" to define them. When times turned difficult, money ran low, friends became scarce, doubt emerged, and haters proliferated, the overwhelming majority of those she profiled refused to "go home." The challenges they faced could not destroy their confidence. I pray you are made of the same mettle.

In summation, the route of "go home," while easily imagined, proves difficult to navigate because of several realities: 1) the glorious work of God in the spiritual realm; 2) the indomitable human spirit; 3) the overriding American ethos; and, 4) the allure of the "go big" spirit.

Let's close with consideration to those four benefits, and our responses.

You must not "go home" because of

1) The Glorious Work of God in the Spiritual Realm

Absent a memorandum from God declaring your end, you must press on, persevere, continue in the fight, stay in the race, and keep up the faith until . . . those in spiritual relationship with God through Christ are resilient. A friend once preached a message with this primary emphasis: "As long as God works *up there,* Christians must worship, pray, fast, and work *down here.*"

When I speak of God, I affirm the biblical God, the holy, awesome, personal Creator and Sustainer of the universe, especially sovereign and transcendent over humanity, governments, leaders, systems, fish, fowl, animals, and all of nature.

Let me be clear: I am not equating God with the incomprehensible notion of the "universe," "the man upstairs," "a spirit," the innocuous "the One," or any other generic rendering of the almighty God. Rather, I reference the self-existent God who revealed Himself as recorded in the inspired, infallible, inerrant, authoritative Scriptures, culminating in His Son, Jesus Christ. In Scripture, He (please note that pronoun is capitalized!) presents Himself as the omniscient, omnipresent, omnipotent heavenly Father.

A colleague who attended an Ivy League seminary informed me that his professor forbade him from referring to God in the masculine gender for theological and linguistic reasons, threatening him with a failing grade. Praise God, I am not a product of that seminary, coming under the influence of that nonsensical professor!

The reason I feel supremely confident calling God my heavenly Father is because He answers me whenever I pray in the name of Jesus. Intelligent people (even Christian seminary professors!) should acknowledge the same reality.

And as a Christian principle, our God works mysteriously, meticulously, and miraculously in the spiritual realm. The kingdom of God represents incomparable, indispensable, incomprehensible truth centered in Christ. Those who don't understand the spiritual realm need the new birth experience so they can then process truth from a decidedly supernatural perspective. When and what we don't understand, we trust God for the full and final explanation. Christians live "by faith" (see Romans 1:17).

Faced with the option of "go home," unusual achievement meets those willing to knock, to push, to stretch, to sweat, to hurt, to agonize, to consider quitting, to conceive failure, yet never yield to any temporary setback. That's why the Bible serves as our relentless coach. That's why Christ represents the template for faithfulness to God's assignment. That's why the Spirit of God goads saints toward godliness.

Consider the Word: "be steadfast, immovable, always abounding in the work of the Lord, knowing that your toil is not *in* vain in the Lord" (1 Corinthians 15:58).

2) The Indomitable Human Spirit

Millions are disinclined to embrace the "go home" focus also because something deep within the human psyche refuses to capitulate to adverse circumstances. Something within many of us rises up when we are faced with major challenges. Of course for many, that inner drive, that internal spirit, can be doused by the immensity of what buffets them. Hopefully, that trek toward depression will be thwarted by mental tapes (like music CDs) playing in your mind, reminding you of limitless personal assets.

When you feel overwhelmed, you must announce to yourself in the urban vernacular, "I ain't going out like that!" That's a declaration of the indomitable human spirit. Indeed, you are tougher than you give yourself credit.

Evidence of the indomitable human spirit is vividly displayed as many lose employment, watch pension plans become depleted, face foreclosures, navigate bankruptcy, recover from divorce, battle illnesses, lose friendships, bury loved ones, and endure countless other personal challenges, yet you continue!

A major theme in reading accounts of military engagements like the Civil War, World War I, World War II, Desert Storm, and in places like Korea, Vietnam, Iraq, or Afghanistan is that, faced with tough odds on unfamiliar terrain, often against unfamiliar tactics, U.S. soldiers maintained courage under fire. That's the indomitable human spirit at work. That's admirable about soldiers, as they fight for a cause greater than themselves. That's what produces awards for valor and patriotism.

While I advise employing enhanced intelligence, greater diplomacy, economic sanctions, and wise exit strategies, there are clear cases when war is justified (after the 9/11 attacks on America, for instance). What drives soldiers and armies, as capitulation threatens, is something profound in the human spirit. It's in you!

Most of all, I want the commander-in-chief, military generals, Congress, and other leaders to have skin in the game, risking the lives of their children, grandchildren, or social class as frontline soldiers rather than sending young black, brown, and poor white ones off to possibly die for an unexplained, ill-advised cause. Those who join the military can advance in life through their service to America and other ways.

I pray God will produce tough, tenacious, determined young people throughout the twenty-first century, ones endowed with this indomitable human spirit. And parents must not encourage the "go home" inclination prevalent among so many. Perhaps part of what explains young adults' still residing with parents is the tendency of kind parents to make home overly comfortable for those who should be self-reliant. A word to the wise: among birds, at some point, the long-comfortable nest should in time be unsettled for those ready to fly on their own.

3) The Overriding American Ethos

A third consideration blocking the "go home" impulse is the overriding American ethos. Something deep in the DNA of Americans holds that, despite the circumstances of the moment, things will eventually and inevitably turn out for our betterment.

Perhaps immigrants from diverse countries risk all to reach America, reasoning that even impoverished in America, they are infinitely better off than they would be in their native lands. Indeed, the promise of America infuses Lady Liberty's torch as she claims, "Give me your tired, your poor, your huddled masses yearning to breathe free, the wretched refuse of your teeming shore. Send these, the homeless, the tempest-tossed to me, I lift my lamp beside the golden door!"

So, that welcoming beacon on New York's Ellis Island reverberates across America, fostering broad dreams of freedom, democracy, peace, security, identity, and economic vitality. Immigrants help shape the mosaic of America. For more than two hundred years, they have arrived in this country with boundless optimism, convinced that America is the epic venue for "go big" thinkers.

The story of America, then, refutes any notion of small ambitions. Instead, it could be persuasively argued that the richness of this country rests in its repudiation of limits. Citizens here push boundaries, explore possibilities, and defy odds while expecting great outcomes.

4) The Allure of the "Go Big" Spirit

Simply stated, "Go big" contradicts "go home" because the former is more relevant to achievement.

If you consider the work required to remain in dire straits, relishing painful memories, broken, busted, and disgusted, languishing in negativity, I would suggest you exert more effort to extricate yourself from the mess. It reminds me of the following amusing anecdote of determined progress.

A man swam in a dirty, snake-infested, foul-smelling lake, only making it to the halfway point. Thoroughly discouraged by his perceived inability to make it all the way across, he turned and swam back to shore. It was the same distance as going all the way. To quit halfway is to miss the thrill of going all the way!

So many simply lack discipline, nerve, or perseverance to reach their goals.

As a major prod to continuing and completing our Christian walk of faith, I often tell our congregation, "You must achieve your objective because you have already passed through the toughest part."

Earlier I mentioned my high school, John C. Fremont High School, in Los Angeles, California. As I stated, it was located in the teeming inner city alongside all the known social pathologies (drugs, gangs, violence, shootings, graffiti, broken families, despair). Our school immortalized an American pioneer. That pioneering connection led to its motto: "Find a way or make one." Proudly, we were (and are!) the pathfinders. Daily, that "go big" spirit spurs me toward unusual achievement.

So propelled by God's grace, Christ, God's Spirit, my conversion, the Word, faith, worship, prayer, family, friends, mentors, and all that He has blessed me with, I am unalterably moving toward the paradigm of "go big." Come with me!

Faced with the flawed facets of the "go home" ethos, I cannot understand anyone embracing it as a formula for a successful life. Instead, that mentality should be shunned, forsaken, and thoroughly repudiated. You were born for more; you have been exposed to more. Now, you must achieve more!

In the end, I recall words from a mentor directed to me as a teenager: "If you can't take it, you won't make it; and not many will care if you don't make it."

For the purposes of our discussion in this book, he was telling me that if I chose the "go home" route, my life would never make a difference. Instead, I would have joined the legions of those whose promise was never fulfilled. Indeed, had I chosen that path, this book would not be in your hands!

CHAPTER 3

Go Big: Assessing Knowledge and Skill Sets

If you aspire toward significant achievement—embracing the "go big" sentiment—you must thoroughly assess your personal skill set. Ask yourself, "What do I do well?" "Where am I most competent?" "What am I really qualified to do?" "What employable skills do I possess?" "What will others compensate me for doing in this economy?" "What do I do or can I do that can be marketed and sold to others?"

The assessment will help you gauge your position in the areas of utility, value, and relevance. In short, utility refers to your ability to benefit an employer because of your knowledge, skills, and expertise. Closely tied to that, value measures how you can strengthen, improve, or increase the productivity of a company or individual that hires you. Still in this connection, relevance affirms your ability to quickly adapt to changing circumstances, challenges, and the world around you.

Often, if you are not careful you will try to obtain employment in an area for which you are not designed nor in which you are particularly competent. That's why you need to properly evaluate your knowledge base and skill set.

For example, my wife leads the Human Relations (HR) department for Kansas City (Missouri) Public Schools. With integrity, professionalism, sensitivity, and discretion, she and her team analyze applicants' education, expertise, background, credentials, certifications, letters of recommendations, skill sets, and more in order to place them in positions commensurate with those areas. As such, they should not hire a teacher who does not possess valid teaching credentials, nor an administrator without proven management skills. Nor should they hire aides or custodians without basic skills and abilities commensurate with the job under consideration.

Moreover, in this day of questionable ethics every applicant for any position (coach, educator, manager, politician, even aspiring minister!) in any area should file professional applications with accuracy. Be assured of this: companies of various sizes will scrutinize every résumé item. If you didn't graduate from a particular school or didn't attend a series of classes or conferences as stated on the résumé, you should not claim those credentials. When (not "if") your credentials or skill sets are deemed inaccurate by an HR representative, you will be seen as an unworthy applicant, a fraud unworthy of trust and responsibilities.

Here is the bigger point. If by the grace of God you are an affable, widely exposed, witty applicant that is a gifted communicator able to display your abilities, stop right there. Tell the truth regarding all that can be fact-checked. Again, don't inflate your résumé.

In order to expand the middle class, the backbone of America, employers ask that technical schools and community colleges design training programs that will broaden skills for all willing workers. Once you obtain such skills and connect them with available employment through applying your best efforts, you should realize greater benefits and opportunities in your life. Moreover, gaining employment for which you are qualified will enhance your self-esteem and self-worth. While work will always carry with it a sense of routine and drudgery, it will also bring personal fulfillment when your skills align with your responsibilities. This alignment enables the "go big" ethos to be realized.

At the same time, globalization has opened coveted fields to a much wider pool of job applicants, some of them not even Americans. Foreign workers with particular knowledge bases and skill sets may be selected for positions well before native-born citizens.

In twenty-first-century America amid racial, ethnic, and cultural diversity, people offering multiple skills and abilities, with millions more coming to our shores, you should recognize that recent citizens (or undocumented workers) have done well by any measure.

Increasingly, the ranks of nannies, maids, landscapers, taxi drivers, small contractors, agricultural laborers, and more are occupied by immigrants from all over the world. Often, these tough jobs are deemed by native-born Americans as beneath them. On the other hand, immigrants (legal and otherwise) view the same jobs as entry-level to their dreams of middle-class status in America.

In a relatively short span of time, with a practical strategy some of these immigrants own homes, start businesses, pay taxes, vote regularly, enroll their children in athletic programs, and attend civic events while steadily rising in the American melting pot.

A late 2014 presidential executive order offered undocumented persons several paths to work and, eventually, citizenship. Not surprisingly, it is estimated that more than five million affected by this order will experience a wide range of opportunities. Indeed, mass deportation of the roughly twelve million such persons is unethical, impractical, and beyond the scope of the government's capabilities.

Let the occupational/economic facts sink in: If an estimated twelve million undocumented workers in America were somehow deported to their home countries, it would create a void in the service industry, manual labor industry, and in the skilled labor sector. At present, some jobs are preferred while others are assailed. Foreign-born workers take the jobs assailed by some, on their path toward the American dream of prosperity.

America's largest state, California (with 30 million residents), offers a stark illustration of the degree to which immigrants are integral to the U.S. economy. Consider this state as a microcosm of the phenomenon of millions of new workers.

In Southern California, many immigrants are hotel maids, garment workers, private housekeepers, nannies, and landscapers, performing what some would term menial jobs yet undergirding the U.S. economy for millions. These persons work long and hard hours, yet these are jobs few native-born Americans would want.

In the San Joaquin-Central Valley (Bakersfield, Merced, Visalia, and Fresno), the vast majority of laborers who harvest crops are undocumented. Their status represents America's open secret. No serious politician (even from the conservative extreme) would publicly argue for sending them back home! And, given the greater economic options in this sector of America's economy, self-deportation seems a ridiculous notion.

In Silicon Valley, the same dynamic is at work at the opposite end of the spectrum, with a decidedly different outcome. There, immigrants bring a wealth of knowledge in specialized disciplines (science, technology, engineering, and mathematics). These highly skilled immigrants receive favored visas and expedited opportunities for U.S. citizenship. The other dirty little secret in Silicon Valley is there is a monochromatic, male-dominated workforce in the tech industry (few black or female workers). All should commend the social justice advocacy of the Rev. Jesse Jackson and others to highlight this vast disparity in a critical U.S. industry. The true picture of the American workforce should reflect the diversity of America, given skill sets commensurate with available jobs.

So, instead of fighting against more immigrants coming to America, fearful of their taking jobs and opportunities away from native-born citizens, we should consider how the economy benefits from those already here. The demagogic rhetoric of billionaire President Donald Trump, notwithstanding, we need the contributions of all Americans. By one estimate, undocumented workers have contributed $100 billion to Social Security over the span of a decade, without any intention of collecting benefits. At the state and local level, households headed by undocumented workers paid another $11 billion in taxes in 2010 alone. If these workers, moreover, were given work permits and brought into the fullness of the American economy, they would contribute $45 billion over the span of five years in payroll taxes, according to a study by the Center for American Progress.

Let me offer a further example of the new world in which we live. In fulfillment of far-flung ministerial obligations, I travel the country regularly. Often in other cities, I need ground transportation by taxicab. In 85 percent of those rides—in cities as different as New York; Richmond, Virginia; Birmingham, Alabama; Miami, Florida; Dallas, Texas; Los Angeles, California; Houston, Texas; Nashville, Tennessee; Cincinnati, Ohio; Kansas City, Missouri; San Francisco, California; Seattle, Washington; and all points in between—the cab drivers have been recent immigrants to America. While in the cab, I query these persons. Here are a few observations:

1) Achievers, by Assessing Skills, Begin at the Bottom with Plans for Success

In my nonscientific, anecdotal interviews, not one cab driver envisioned remaining a cab driver forever. Instead, this was the first rung on a conceptualized ladder of success. Armed with a plan, they toiled in heavy traffic, picking up passengers from the airport. Then they transported riders to various hotels, restaurants, and other destinations.

With a built-in GPS system in their vehicles, they navigated new cities and neighborhoods.

In my simple interviews, I have met men from several African countries, some from Middle Eastern countries, and some from South America. Starting in New York City, Washington, D.C., Philadelphia, or some similar East Coast locale, many migrated across America, some settling even in the Midwest, depending on family ties or the prospect of better economic opportunities. Always, however, these foreign-born workers possessed a clear, definite, practical plan for success.

For some, driving a taxicab represented a true step down in prestige, title, compensation, status, and perks as contrasted with their professions in their native land. Indeed, I have met former engineers, professors, or physicians who found themselves, through a multitude of events and circumstances, driving a cab in America. Moreover, due to political repression, caste systems, tribal warfare, lack of freedoms, and more, some left their native land in search of brighter prospects.

It is astounding that these recent immigrants are undaunted by the challenges of learning a new language, absorbing a new culture, and navigating new laws in a land thousands of miles away from home. The 1988 Eddie Murphy movie *Coming to America* resonates on many levels, revealing the hunger of people of many nationalities for broader opportunities and greater exposure to different and numerous cultures. And, in that particular case, the African prince found a beautiful, American wife!

Several persons in the immigrant category expressed the time-honored tradition of getting their children admitted to America's finest institutions of higher learning. The parent's sentiment was, "Once my child graduates from college or university, going on to professional attainment, he/she will not have to toil in menial employment (as a cab driver, maid, and the like)." Not surprisingly, some of these children, driven by the value of educational emphasis inculcated by parents, become valedictorians of their college classes, surpassing native-born students (both black and white).

I reiterate the immigrant plan: over time through hard work, resilience, budgeting, thriftiness, and more, individuals purchase homes and start businesses while rising in civic engagement. They then represent the prototypical American success story, moving from rags to riches from their arrival and after just one generation. As long-time fight promoter Don King used to say, such a rise is possible "only in America."

Increasingly, these newcomers to America bring with them a cultural framework, work ethic, value system, determination, and persistence, seeing manifold opportunities that native-born Americans take for granted. If they must begin at the proverbial bottom, they acknowledge it as a temporary condition. Given time, working with family members and friends, they pool their resources and live with others to properly position themselves for future advancement.

In realization of the "go big" ideal, native-born Americans, in my view, can learn invaluable lessons from the immigrants' experience as they outwork, out-sacrifice, and out-save many of us born in America. Precisely because we take our political freedoms and economic opportunities for granted, we might well discover one day that our aspirations will continually elude us until we take decisive action.

2) Achievers Are Keenly Aware of Their Skill Sets

While this writer wishes all persons in this country would aspire toward, gain admission to, and graduate from America's best schools, even Ivy League ones, the reality is that not all people relish the same path for success. I really view the notion that some persons are not college material as condescending.

Equally true, I hate the sense that America endorses a caste system, groups of haves, have-nots, and "have-mores," repudiating our classless society. (I laugh as many theorists and intellectuals discuss income inequality absent a solution requiring greater personal preparation.) In short, a confluence of divine grace, education, personal initiative, skills acquisition, government intervention, and morality will change income inequality.

In my judgment, seeking to move up to another level without a workable plan is hollow, foolish, and unrealistic. Some in American culture (even Christian prosperity preachers!) sell pipe dreams when they celebrate ill-considered ventures.

We need to share a necessary dose of economic reality: without intellectual preparation, native athleticism, vocal abilities, acting chops, entrepreneurial gifting, or some other personal quirk, this world considers some useless for marketable, true, and sustained achievement. Consider that early twenty-first-century millionaires and billionaires are technology innovators, exceptional athletes, visionaries, corporate titans, hedge fund managers, children of wealth, and a few others. Indeed, you are probably not likely to reach such rarified economic status by dint of hard work alone.

Instead, the transition from one level of attainment to another is fueled by hard work, harnessing energy, effort, and engagement. You must passionately pursue a dream, a worthy objective, fulfilling a true mission. Within this matrix, plumbers, for example, will understand their particular skill set. Through hands-on training, going to technical school, making money, and more, they hone critical capacities for ensuring the free flow of the water systems in homes and businesses to the relief and for the convenience of customers. Also, we note others with bona fide skill sets: nurses, technicians, welders, masons, auto mechanics, and others.

For those so inclined, certified cosmetologists work to support proper grooming (hair, feet, nails, and the like) for men and women. In this regard, Americans spend billions annually to look and feel their best, aided by such professionals. I recall how through determination and a strong work ethic, a dedicated hair stylist went from renting one chair to owning the entire salon, with other stylists paying her!

In another area of specialty—automobile maintenance—millions are grateful for those able to discern an errant ping to utilize advanced technological systems to discover what to do about it. As a young man, my older brothers taught me the basics of auto care: changing oil filters, gaskets, tires, rims, starters, solenoids, replacing radiators, and more. Today, I gladly defer to the knowledge of professionals working at the car dealership.

The American economy is vibrant and individual lives more fulfilled as millions identify their special skill sets. Once you identify yours, the future appears brighter!

With the right skill set, welders, plumbers, nurses, mechanics, and others can, with hard work, dedication, grit, and faith, reap solidly middle-class compensation, realizing all the benefits of the American dream: home ownerships, health care, vehicles, pensions, vacations, savings for children's college expenses, and more.

3) Hard Work Fuels the Achievement of Those Willing to Apply Themselves

American business lore is filled with accounts of those who founded small companies with little more than an idea, grit, and a hunch. Then they put in long hours and watched as increased capital allowed for better equipment and larger facilities, while new specialties converged. In time, this small venture of, say, five employees parlayed their work into millions in annual revenue. The one truck became ten trucks as account receivables increased. Through innovations derived from sweat equity, employing family members early on, going beyond the capacity of competitors, such entrepreneurs succeed beyond anyone's—including their own—imagination.

Indeed, some fifty million American small businesses drive the U.S. economy by employing millions, developing communities, and paying taxes (oh my!) while fueling the entrepreneurial spirit in so many.

In this regard, I aim to chart the outlines of an entrepreneurial plan.

Through keen analysis of their markets, such owners find the right combination of supply to meet demand for their goods or services. Typically, they fill a niche for a product or service that, once it is provided, others find it obvious. Recently, I read the obituary of a man who started an aviation company from the ruins of the old Spruce Goose plane made famous by the reclusive billionaire Howard Hughes. This new aviation company later morphed into a museum, showcasing the plane and its history to a new generation of tourists.

Over time, the phenomenal success of these small companies attracts the attention of major investors. Sometimes they are bought out by larger companies who fold the smaller entity into its corporate mold. The original owners then reap millions in the sale. This windfall thus allows them to go on to new endeavors. At its best, this epitomizes the model of capitalism.

4) Skills Not Correlating to Demands of the Market Require Necessary Changes

A robust debate rages as millions in America view the passage of the old days of willingness to work with perkiness, a strong back, and determination. Now, you need new skills (often technological ones). Lifting furniture and delivering it now requires computerized training. Young men must move beyond merely a high school education.

In the last few years, employers have expressed a desire for a workforce conversant in the so-called STEM areas: science, technology, engineering, and mathematics. In the furtherance of the twenty-first century, those equipped in these disciplines will be sought after as eminently qualified for new jobs.

Increasingly, even the pleasant secretary in an office, once termed a receptionist, who used to blithely answer telephones, must be computer literate to properly route and record incoming calls, while preparing spreadsheets and performing numerous other duties. Also, she or he must navigate the Internet for new sources of information to benefit the company.

So, the preparation for this person involves training and retraining in areas of professional weakness. Ideally, he or she may enroll in a community college, pursuing specific training in information technology (IT). Such an enhanced skill set would open new opportunities, making the employee more valuable to the company. Then, armed with new skills, that person can transition to a new position there. Newly empowered, she or he would accrue other economic and psychological benefits.

5) With All Skill Sets, Be Ready for Change: Keep an Updated Résumé

In the twenty-first-century economy, the workforce will be characterized by the ability to adapt to changes that happen at blinding speed, nimble in the face of constant transition. From multitasking to telecommuting to flexible schedules, adjusting to change is indispensable. Office workers, firefighters, police officers, nurses, managers, and others must constantly adapt to a new work paradigm.

If you presently work in one of the aforementioned areas, the best advice for you sounds simple: read, learn more, develop capabilities, strive for additional knowledge, take the plunge, ask God for more opportunities, and then soar like a bird!

Moreover, whereas the generation aged 70-plus celebrated working at one job/plant/site/company for thirty years before retirement, the generation between ages 20 and 55 will work at three different jobs or three different companies over the same time frame.

So you will probably transition through several jobs before reaching the age or stage of retirement. As many benefits and perks may be transferred from one company to another, there is not the sense of lost time or energy. In fact, a layoff may be interpreted as a greater opportunity to diversify your skill set, giving you more favorable experience in the work world.

An updated résumé will express the multiple experience and skills you possess. Human resource personnel seek to ascertain an applicant's adaptability to an ever-changing job market. They wonder, "Are you a first-class, proven team player, exuding competence, discipline, professionalism, punctuality, reliability, responsibility, loyalty, and other qualities?

To embrace the "go big" ethos, then, you must appraise your skill set. Ask yourself, "Does my skill set equate with the available jobs and economy of today?"

If yes, then get ready for your impending life adventure. If not, develop a better plan for engagement. Keep reading for more that will fuel your trek toward all that encapsulates the "go big" lifestyle.

6) Achievers Obtain Skills Commensurate with the Employment Landscape

In the twenty-first-century world, the best skills for the employment landscape involve STEM capabilities, marketing, data analysis, and computer programming. Proficiency in any one or more of those disciplines will mean steady employment, regardless of ethnicity, background, or physical differences.

When they deem themselves inadequate in a field of knowledge or lacking in necessary skills, most intelligent people will seek to increase their knowledge and broaden their skills. I know that you are in that intelligent category.

Accordingly, technical schools and community colleges offer courses and training in critical areas like web and applications development and programming languages. When your résumé illustrates such skills, HR professionals tend to salivate as you sit before them. In you, they see someone who, with necessary training for a specific job, will prove invaluable to the company's workforce.

As I encourage the "go big" spirit, you may assess the validity of returning to school after years in the workforce. Logic dictates that if you aspire toward better outcomes, you must enhance your knowledge and skills. Remember: you are never too old to learn new skills. People in so-called MOOC (massive open online courses) are just as old, tired, and overwhelmed by responsibilities as you are. The difference is they really want more for their lives. Yet, I do not expect anything less of you!

Chapter 4

Go Big: Self-confidence and Optimism

Self-confidence has been badly maligned over the last few years, as some have interpreted it to mean arrogant disregard for others. Self-confidence also has been identified as the motivator of those seeking to get ahead to take advantage of others. In this way, we think of shysters, schemers, charlatans, corrupt leaders, crooks, and other conmen. Because of their slick presentations, glib demeanor, quick wit, A-type personality, charm, charisma, and accoutrements of success, many have fallen prey to various cons. Think of investment guru Bernard Madoff, whose scheming ruined lives and squandered pensions, only to land him a 150-year prison sentence. Such represents a sentence of life in prison, as Madoff currently is in his seventies!

Properly understood, however, self-confidence represents an attractive quality when it is coupled with the sovereignty of God. Let me quickly make the case. God is ultimately in control of your life. By grace, He allows you to use personal talents, education, and experiences to make choices aided by considerations, which lead to consequences.

1) Self-confidence Empowers You

Confidence fuels passion for the "go big" mentality because you must believe that what you attempt will be successful, if it is to become successful. Nothing beneficial or lasting emanates from pessimism, negativity, fatalism, or the range of ways you may personally block your own great accomplishments.

When self-confidence and optimism intertwine, you exemplify necessary strategies for reaching higher. Because everyday existence exposes you to the fullness of bad external challenges, you need vast internal reserves. In life's battles, you may become an unwitting or unwilling casualty because you did not confidently stand against the onslaught. In other words, when confidence and optimism converge, you start planning for when the battle is over!

Moved by the necessity of "go big" being fully achieved in you and through you, you are supremely expectant of victory no matter the odds, obstacles, or obstructions. You view each hindrance as only temporary. That obstruction must move because it prevents the seizing of territory that has been earmarked for you. It's yours if you reach for it.

I am mystified by persons who can perceive a great blessing can be for someone as if that person was entitled to it. Yet, when it comes to the person himself, he disqualifies himself. Let me cite an example. Some Christian colleagues lead large, thriving ministries with several thousand parishioners. As for me, God has given me more than enough congregants for the advancement of the kingdom of God through Christ in my local setting. As all the body of Christ works from the same side using the same Bible, affirming the same Christ as Lord, fighting only the enemy of the righteous, I am neither intimidated by nor envious of spiritual colleagues leading large fellowships.

Frankly, as every Christian leader operates in divine grace, I have never felt that another was more worthy or more godly or more gifted or more prayerful or holier than I, thus attributing the difference in congregational size. In fact, in theological terms, God acts in grace, giving more to one, less to another, all by His sovereign will.

My counsel to myself (and others) is very simple: use all of your gifts and talents for the glory of God in advancing His kingdom through the risen Savior, Jesus Christ. Then, leave the essentials of your success plan to the perfect will of God. Indeed, some will lead large ministries with national and global acclaim while others will bless small Christian fellowships far from the glare of notoriety. Before God, each Christian leader will be held accountable for the outcome of the ministry he/she led in a lifetime of service.

2) Self-confidence Celebrates Your Place in the World

In Christian ministry, the grace of God places one at one site while placing another in a different venue, all for His greater glory. Since God is sovereign He can choose, without your permission, to assign one Christian leader five thousand parishioners, while giving another eighty-five congregants, with equal love for each. Indeed, you should love, lead, teach, protect, preach, counsel, pray for, and serve the mission of Jesus Christ, irrespective of the size, history, influence, locale, or financial asset base of your particular ministry.

A related truth must be emphasized: many Christians mistake financial riches and material prosperity as indicators of true godliness or success. Forthrightly, Paul addressed this matter in 1 Timothy 6. In the context of this passage, there are false teachers who sought remunerative gain and so justified their insatiable greed by describing gain as a measure of God's favor. Paul rejected this notion in the strongest terms, disputing that the blessing hand of God is seen primarily in financial or material terms.

Currently, there are those Christian leaders who teach (erroneously, in my view) that a person's value to others is defined by his or her material worth. My buddy Bishop Kenneth Ulmer holds that personal worth is too often the gauge by which we evaluate a person's value to God and His kingdom. Conversely, Paul says in 1 Timothy 6:6 that the goal for Christians, greater than gold, represents godliness accompanied by contentment.

The key concept to consider in your walk with God should be godliness with contentment. *Contentment* means appropriate deference to God as the source for all you have while striving for the greater in areas that are within His will, using whatever you have for the advancement of the kingdom of God. That objective reveals wealth, true prosperity, and lasting riches. Accordingly, you must assiduously reject the notion of the corrupted Golden Rule: "He who has the gold rules."

Moreover, I encourage you to repudiate the dangerous idea (even among immature Christians) of "getting all we can, canning all we get, and sitting on the can," while millions lack resources sufficient for their immediate needs.

What I mean is simple: as Sovereign, God chooses individuals (wholly through His choosing) to lead His followers. All are uniquely called, anointed, gifted, and assigned by Him to the place where He will be glorified as they share Jesus Christ.

3) Using Your Gifting from God

So every servant of God must evaluate himself/herself on the basis of faithful utilization of all the gifts, talents, specialties, expertise, and abilities given by God for His glory. As instruments in God's hands, none makes a lasting difference without His work in and through us.

Put another way, every Christian leader—no matter how insightful, scholarly, profound, "deep," or whatever—represents, at best, a lifeless dummy on the lap of the Master Ventriloquist. Ultimate glory should go to the One who invisibly animates that dummy. So while I take God, His people, and His kingdom objectives quite seriously, I don't take myself as seriously.

Let me apply another coat of polish to this matter. Early in my marriage, I was invited to share the message for a large community's Martin Luther King Jr. Birthday Celebration. This was a coveted preaching spot; I was new to the area. As I do always, I prayed, studied, and worked very hard on that message. Befitting Dr. King, I aimed for rhetoric of the highest caliber. After hearing me deliver it, my loving wife said, "Babe, you were really good tonight. I saw you in a different light. You are a really gifted speaker."

With self-confidence tempered by the recognition of God's grace, I replied, "I am so glad you now see in me what I have seen in myself for years. I sincerely hope many others will get that same news flash."

Now, you must assess my comment. If you think it borders on swagger, pride, or too much self-confidence, that's fine with me. If you understand it and apply it to your life, realizing your full potential, then, I thank God.

Today, you need self-confidence and optimism to conquer the multiple challenges of this life: "Am I attractive enough? Smart enough? Talented enough? Will they like me? Do I have something worth adding to the matter? Can I say it properly? Will they laugh at me?"

4) The perennial Battle of Insecurity

While each person must answer such questions personally, let me offer a word to all: every person—even celebrities, athletes, corporate leaders, politicians, all—grapples with personal insecurities. Most, however, mask their insecurities through boasting, bravado, glibness, fashion, jewelry, homes, vehicles, stocks, mutual funds, trusts, yachts, private jets, exotic vacations, bodyguards, money, verbosity, charisma, wit, or their special skills in a given arena.

My advice is straight-forward when faced with a new challenge, particularly in a professional or personal setting: get up, pray, dress appropriately, eat, review the situation, see yourself in the matter, collect your thoughts, be punctual, and meet the situation, all while concealing any anxiety, as it is common to all humanity. After all, several wags have theorized that 80 percent of the task involves merely showing up! The other 20 percent involves the grace of God, self-confidence, optimism, attire, vocabulary, preparation, bearing, and your resolute striving.

This advice applies to a date with a prospective romantic partner, as well as a job interview. Remember, the other party is just as nervous as you are. The other party (even the HR representative) also wants to make a favorable impression. Remember: the company needs your abilities, even as you are seeking personal fulfillment. Each has a vested interest in a successful outcome.

Once, a friend said, "People can sense and smell fear. It is pungent!" Apply that truth by cleansing yourself in the refreshing waters of optimism and self-confidence.

5) "Why Not Me?" Thoughts

If you aspire to the "go big" level, it will require an adjustment in your self-evaluation. Over and again, ask yourself, "Why not me?"

- "Why not me, owning my own business?"
- "Why not me, enjoying a healthy, loving relationship?"
- "Why not me, drug-free, sober, and reflective?"
- "Why not me, graduating from college/university?"
- "Why not me, advancing in a professional career?"
- "Why not me, living free of personal drama and dysfunction?"
- "Why not me, owning my own home and building wealth for the future?"
- "Why not me, saving and investing for my and my family's future?"
- "Why not me, encouraging my children in healthy, affirming pursuits?"
- "Why not me, celebrating positive accomplishments?"
- "Why not me, committing to God-honoring marriage and stability?"

- "Why not me, healthy in body, mind, and spirit?"
- "Why not me, washed in the blood of Jesus, living for Him, in regular worship?"
- "Why not me, giving the Lord's tithe while supporting Christian ministries?"
- "Why not me, praying, studying the Word, living holy, and sharing Christ?"
- "Why not me, fulfilled, joyful, and engaging?"

6) Transform Your Thinking

This matter of self-confidence transforms your thinking, taking you to the heights of "go big." Indeed, that "it" (whatever you desire to achieve) won't happen for you unless and until you visualize yourself in it.

Envision yourself in a better scenario, a better marriage, a better economic level, a better objective, a better life mission, with different friends/associates, moving to a better understanding of God and His will for your life. The little cute phrase I often offer audiences holds true: "If you can conceive it, visually perceive it, firmly believe it, while working hard to achieve it, God, ultimately, will honor it!"

If you really want to exercise self-confidence and optimism, you should take a lesson from a reputed conquistador who, arguably, may have been history's greatest example of the "go big" mentality.

7) "Burn the Ships"

On February 19, 1519, Spanish conquistador Hérnan Cortés landed in Mexico on the shores of the Yucatan peninsula. With an entourage of 11 ships, 13 horses, 110 sailors, and 553 soldiers, he maintained one driving passion: seize the great treasures of gold known to be in that area. The indigenous population upon his arrival was approximately five million.

In this venture, Cortés and his men were facing considerable odds: previous expeditions had failed; they were unfamiliar with the area; they would need to fight those defending the gold; the weather was challenging; and they had insufficient supplies. Nothing seemed favorable!

With all this in mind, Cortés recognized the necessity of summoning unusual courage from his shipmates and soldiers. Somehow, he had to boost flagging morale. He had already persuaded five hundred men to venture with him over the seas on eleven rickety ships.

Cortés understood that this mercenary task required all or nothing from all involved. Accordingly, he told his men the following: "We can defeat the enemy. This treasure belongs to the strong. We must give this effort our all. Let us burn all our ships. If we fail, we will die, or return to Spain on our enemy's ships."

Burn the ships! That was the plan!

In the annals of recorded military history, it was a shrewd motivational ploy designed to underline the nature of full commitment to any task. This was the epitome of strategic conceptualization, the optimal tactical deployment. Cortés surmised that if his soldiers had no way home, they would then not have failure as an option; thus, they would fight with unprecedented tenacity.

Amazingly, Cortés and his men conquered the Aztec fighters, capturing the gold, succeeding beyond their wildest dreams, and achieving where others had failed in six centuries of attempts.

What can we learn from this example? The following are a few lessons:

8) Achievers Abandon Excuses, Crutches, or Reasons for Failure

Listening to the recounting of this story, none can doubt the supreme self-confidence and optimism of Cortés. Leaders, then, matter! When they embrace the "go big" idea, they influence others around them by their sheer audacity and by the sway of their certainty. The task ahead is made easier because of the confluence of these ideas.

Clearly, Cortés and his men knew the challenges they faced. By all reasoning, they should have abandoned their dreams of fortune and gone home. They could have congratulated themselves on simply starting the venture. Many had not gotten that far. Or they could have rationalized that six centuries of quests had proven futile, thus resigning themselves to thinking that procuring the gold was impossible! Or, they could have reveled in the excuse of inadequate supplies: "Maybe if we had been better prepared, we could have prevailed." Indeed, any excuse will suffice if fear is present.

Moreover, Cortés's crew could have remained comfortable in complacency, unwilling to risk failure on the open seas in a time fraught with inhumanity, larceny, greed, and duplicity. In such a corrupt milieu with disease, destruction, deception, and death as rampant possibilities, they would have been within their rights to mutiny against Cortés: "Sorry, Captain, we're heading back to Spain."

Today, excuses impede progress and negate victories because, most often, you are justified in your excuses. And others usually acknowledge the validity of your excuses. So, excuse makers enjoy the company of other excuse makers, and the negative cycle continues.

Disappointingly, personal excuses become crutches. The usual benefit of a crutch is that it is an aid for walking, a support for a weak hip, knee, ankle, or leg. When you fail to walk at all, depending fully on the crutch, it inhibits the rehabilitative process. Likewise, excessive excuse making functions like a crutch, thwarting your accomplishment.

For a recent example of abandoning excuses, throwing away crutches, and refusing to allow clear dangers to thwart progress, consider the long-shot presidential campaign of Barack Obama in 2008. At the time, Obama was a young, inexperienced, unknown former community organizer in Chicago, former state senator in Illinois, and a freshman U.S. senator with no great legislative legacy. Add to this that he was facing a much better-known field of Democratic candidates: former First Lady Hillary Clinton; well-established U.S. senator, Joe Biden; former Clinton cabinet member and former New Mexico governor, Bill Richardson; former vice-presidential nominee John Edwards; another well-regarded U.S. senator, Chris Dodd; and others.

Perhaps we should move past the most obvious obstacle: Obama was black and, therefore, would be the first black candidate with a real chance to gain the nomination. If successful there, he would then face a strong Republican candidate (a war hero!) in the November 2008 election.

As was alluded to in an earlier chapter, Barack Hussein Obama (even he calls it a funny name) achieved the ultimate "go big" in

American politics and in American history, being elected America's forty-fourth president, becoming the first black occupant of the White House. In 2012, he was reelected. By any measure, these feats were supra-achievements.

Like Cortés the conquistador, Obama the candidate, in order to be successful, had to "burn the ships!"

Similarly, if you aspire toward a significant milestone (career, relationship, promotion, college degree), you must be prepared to act accordingly: "Burn the ships!"

If you really want life to blossom before you, burn the ships of past failure and past success. Neither ship will carry you to your new destination.

Also, you must burn the ship of negative self-esteem. As stated earlier, why not you?

Burn the ship of depression. Whatever "it" is, it must not pull you under its sway. Make a commitment to yourself: "This" (whatever the distraction) will not define, describe, or destroy me!

Burn the ship of "loser" friends. You can fail alone!

Burn the ship of bad habits. The right habit—started, evaluated, and continued—will nullify previous bad ones.

Burn the ship of procrastination. Now is your moment!

Burn the ship of negativity. Walk in the brilliance of positive optimism.

Burn the ship of regret. Yesterday represents a yellowed page in your diary. Today affirms your opportunity to succeed in a worthy endeavor. Burn the ship of anguish/guilt over a long-ago, ill-advised indiscretion. By now, God has forgiven you while compassionate people have forgotten it. Now, release yourself from its tentacles.

While you're at it, burn the ship of your old way of life.

9) Take Possession of Your Narrative

Indeed, if unlimited success is to be your possession, establishing your legacy, you must willingly "burn the ships!" This is the process of taking authority of your narrative.

In a word, never allow others to write your story. None should be granted the right to determine your success or failure. Often, you have heard it said, "If not for that relationship, I would be much better off in life." Perhaps you have made a similar comment. If so, please take command of your story! You are more than a series of bad choices, a victim of wrong decisions, a slave to foolish moments. Indeed, those things may be descriptive, but they don't have to be definitive. Let me explain.

The old aphorism captures it well: *"Fool me once, shame on you. Fool me twice, shame on me."* In the former, you were a victim of the machinations of another; in the latter, you intentionally chose the wrong path.

Jack Welch of GE Corporation fame, shortly after retirement, composed his personal and professional memoirs. He reflected on what he had learned over forty years in "corporate warfare," dealing with boards, shareholders, colleagues, lower-level managers, selling his product, and appearing before Congress all while relating to the general public. Welch would not allow anyone to control his narrative. He was at GE as CEO in difficult times, in exhilarating times, in recessionary times, and he would not allow others to interpret his thinking or decisions in crucial moments. Instead, he would explain these matters of global importance.

I encourage you to place past failures, sin, immorality, poor choices, dumb moments, and regrets on that metaphorical ship. On this imagined ship, with other "passengers" put sadness, false friends, shame, guilt, doubts, and apprehensions. Once they are all comfortably aboard your ship, then symbolically burn it up!

Stand close to the fiery blob. Watch the smoke rise. See the smoldering mess. Wait near it so as to be assured that it's all consumed in the flames. Years of negative stuff are suddenly gone!

The Bible captures the immensity of the undertaking of figuratively burning your ships: "Not that I have already obtained *it* or have already become perfect, but I press on so that I may lay hold of that for which also I was laid hold of by Christ Jesus. . . . but one thing *I do*: forgetting what *lies* behind and reaching forward to what *lies* ahead" (Philippians 3:12, 13).

In other words, those things which were toxic in your mind, debilitating to your psyche, heavy on your heart, and troublesome to your well-being should be consigned to your past. Freed by the pernicious flames, I advise this: experience cleansing release in your heart, mind, spirit, and will. Once your internal recesses are cleansed by the flame, you are now on the way to your "go big" objective.

10) Learn to Interpret Inflection Points

Supreme self-confidence and optimism enabled Cortés the conquistador, Obama the candidate, and Welch the corporate titan to seize the moment. In the process, each learned what would become a crucial turning point for major achievement. In each case, it is possible that well-meaning comrades advised each leader of a better, more propitious time, with greater allies, revenue, experience, and more. That's the difference between success and failure: knowing whose report to believe! Indeed, to achieve at the highest levels, you must "burn the ships" while fighting with bulldog tenacity. Indeed, to avoid the "go home" impulse, you must be resolute in your pursuit!

Without question, life will ratchet up pressure on you, demanding a decision, placing you at a crossroads, the proverbial "fork in the road" which could ultimately determine your life's trajectory.

Moving too early or waiting too late can prove disastrous, with far-reaching implications.

If you sense the "go big" spirit within you, few can interpret when you should make your move. As a Christian pastor, I have been asked by many, "What should I do?" My advice is this: "Really pray about this matter." Once I am assured they have sought God, I encourage the brother or sister in Christ to take the plunge. Of course, I remind all that no one can really discern for you the best moment of the confluence of events. At best, each of us makes our choices with the information available at the time. Hindsight is 20/20; foresight is rare.

Let me engage your imagination at this point. What might Moses have been thinking the night prior to marching into Pharaoh's court, settling his fate when he declared, "Let my people go!"? Did Moses have trepidation? Absolutely. Yet, he went through with the task. Staying with Moses, what was his mental state just before leading God's people across the Red Sea? Or, right before leading them into the vagaries of the wilderness?

In all scenarios, life poses the challenge of what constitutes a crucial decision point. If you want to succeed beyond your wildest dreams, you must in faith seize the moment, integrating all you know, believe, and trust before "crossing the Rubicon." After crossing it, you will know there is no possibility of turning back.

11) Live without a Plan B

If God is your Source (and He should be!), you need to proceed in absolute faith, putting your total plan A on the line. You must realize that, really, there is no plan B. As long as you maintain a plan B, you will be tempted to rely upon it, thus preventing the implementation of plan A, your best course of action.

Let me offer a personal illustration of operating without a plan B. By the grace of God, I was reared by a godly, sainted, single mother, along with my three siblings. Through hard work (as a nurse), loving God, and blessing others, my mother kept us safe, clothed, fed, and in a home of our own. Among African Americans, I thought our family was well off until later when university professors told me I was deprived by urban pathologies!

My mother expected each of her children to succeed according to their exposure, preparation, and inclinations. With good health and focus, she expected each child to acquire the best of education for a life of personal and professional attainment. When I was admitted to a first-class university, she was elated. When I graduated with a bachelor's degree, she counseled me to obtain a master's degree. When I obtained that one, she implored me to go further for a terminal degree, the doctorate. (Though I have several honorary doctorates, I still need to earn a doctoral degree.)

Since I had no plan B (vast inheritance, family business to take over, walk in an established legacy, or bask in perpetual benevolence from a rich uncle) early on, I sensed the necessity of a high-quality education and moral excellence as the route to success and lasting achievement. Without a viable plan B, I had to sincerely trust that God would order my steps and direct my path. (With thirty-eight-plus years of Christian ministry, thirty-three-plus years as a Christian pastor, national preaching acclaim, about ten books published, a loving family, and many friends, a few material possessions, I bless the name of my heavenly Father through Christ for all He has achieved through a yielded vessel.)

Further, one of the realizations of those interested in a professional acting career is that either New York City or Los Angeles must be their destination. In one of those venues, they would discover opportunity, work, fame, focus, and fortune. Success on television, stage, and screen await those willing to stay with their plan A. Despite rejections, ugly encounters, terrible living situations, small parts, waiting tables, parking cars, calls home, internal questions, and general frustration, many prevail through sheer determination.

Elizabeth Taylor, Barbara Streisand, Meryl Streep, Julia Roberts, Taraji P. Henson, Halle Berry, Jack Lemmon, Warren Beatty, Brad Pitt, Tom Cruise, Denzel Washington, Eddie Murphy, Tyler Perry, Samuel L. Jackson, Will Smith, and thousands of others paid their dues in working odd jobs and playing small parts without a plan B. Their resolve in perfecting their craft of acting has produced their Academy Award-winning performances!

In your field, such a resolve can produce similar results. You simply must not countenance or seriously consider operating from a plan B mentality.

Plan A thinking results in plan A results. On the other hand, plan B thinking leads, inevitably, to plan B outcomes.

Here is another example. In 2000, I was called by God from my native Los Angeles to lead an historical, ministry-oriented Christian fellowship in the Midwest. That 1,500-mile trek involved far more than geographic relocation. It also involved a philosophical, "Burn the ships!"

Once there, I discovered a great church family to lead, married a beautiful, talented wife, celebrated the birth of a spirited daughter, enjoyed writing several books, renovated a multifaceted sanctuary, built a forty-three-unit senior facility, fed thousands, engaged with new colleagues, was healed by God of a brain tumor, contributed to national causes, encouraged young people in academic pursuits, ran for political office, and more.

What has happened to me can also happen to you, provided you abandon falling back on plan B if plan A proves challenging.

Freedom in Christ represents vulnerability in God while having nothing else if God fails to provide. Yet, God always provides and prevails over any situation as long as you operate without a plan B.

Self-confidence and optimism are critical guides if you are determined to embrace and live out the tenets of the "go big" philosophy.

If for some reason you lack self-confidence, and if you are overwhelmed by a spirit of pessimism, I want to encourage you with helpful truths.

First, everyone on this planet suffers from doubts, defeats, and disasters. Second, no matter how many times you may have fallen, no matter how many dreams shattered, your best days are always ahead of you. Third, each morning there is a person staring back at you from the mirror whom you must love, forgive, and affirm. Fourth, you are an exact fit in some place; you must find that place. Finally, even amid uncertainty, you must carry out your work.

Indeed, confidence and optimism reveal themselves in your responses to this series of questions:

- What drives you, making it impossible to alter your course?
- What keeps you engaged in a pursuit as others lose focus?
- What deeply disturbs you that others do not otherwise notice?
- What produces indignation in you, while others accept it as life's routine?
- What fosters joy in your soul beyond the norm?

If you sense any of the above resonating in your spirit, it is time—really, past time!—to burn your ships! Keep reading for more torches and kerosene.

CHAPTER 5

Go Big: Drive and Determination

As we walk together on our "go big" journey, you should by now have taken in significant content. The chapters of this book emanate from a series of biblical analyses, long conversations, critical reflection, motivational studies, articles, books, consultations, and observations from the perspective of what makes for unusual attainment. My conclusion: In order to achieve, you must integrate personal drive and determination. We should thoroughly investigate these intertwined notions.

Drive is variously defined as the internal propulsion in the human psyche; that which forces movement; a compelling or constraining force for progress; and to cause and guide the movement toward an intelligible objective.

When you critically examine your life, you must discover your inner drive. You may want to discover what really motivates you. What excites your passion? What can you talk about all night long?

1) The Range of Drives

Some people are driven by expectations of *solid, healthy relationships*. You may be a husband who aims to consistently love and nurture your wife. Or you may be a wife who aims to consistently love, respect, honor, and encourage your husband. In the best scenario, both seek to provide their children with models of integrity, consistency, dignity, kindness, compassion, fairness, and intelligence.

If searching for a mate, you probably intend to meet someone who exemplifies particular traits which align with your own so as to foster a healthy environment, beneficial dialogue, and prudent decisionmaking, which fosters realization of your shared goals.

"Go big" coincides with this expectation, acutely aware that interpersonal relationships matter! Even when people express contentment in single status, something deep within human beings yearns for committed companionship, leading to a defined status. Thus, possessed of the "go big" sensibility, you expect and work for healthy, affirming relationships.

Often, you may be driven by dreams of *immense wealth*, so you work two jobs and save every penny possible after bills are paid. Or you voraciously read business-oriented magazines. Or you might enroll in business classes. Or you might invest in stocks, bonds, and mutual funds. Or you might scour the business section of the newspaper, seeking an edge on others. Or you might scan the Internet for the next big thing, hoping to become filthy rich. Or you might succumb to the seduction of get-rich-quick schemes or con artists. After all that, the median income for an American family is $38,000 annually, hardly the stuff of unfathomable riches.

The "go big" philosophy recognizes in this instance that every person who really studies, really works, really invests, really sacrifices, will experience a discernable increase in wealth generation. While I acknowledge that wealth on the level of an entertainer, athlete, Silicon Valley entrepreneur, hedge fund manager, or private equity executive may not be a reality for all, you can vastly improve your income and wealth by dint of greater knowledge, creative work, longer hours, an investment strategy, and patient sacrifices.

Some people are driven by *dynamic engagement*. You yearn to make life better for others, so you might sacrifice high compensation for the chance to enhance others' lives (public school teachers, for example). Or you might leave America, traveling to distant lands to serve in impoverished countries (think, missionaries or medical personnel). Or feeling guilty about your material comfort, you might give thousands or millions to charitable causes (as a result, your name may be emblazoned on hospital plaques or adorn college buildings). Or sensing an injustice, you might sign up to further a cause (for or against abortion rights; defending vulnerable communities; for or against taxation; breast cancer awareness; saving the planet, and so on). The possibilities are endless, as you seek to leave the world better than you found it.

The "go big" mindset makes its commitment early, entering the arena of social-justice advocacy and enlightened engagement. Indeed, you can seize unlimited opportunities: share your passion for feeding the hungry; help urban and minority youth find employment; help reduce urban violence; support sensible sentencing guidelines; encourage family initiatives; register and organize voters on a particular issue; work in a political campaign; volunteer to tutor young people; or stand against unsafe practices impacting children.

Some are driven by *fears and insecurities*. You might secretly harbor the notion that you will one day die all alone. So you make family the highest priority, aiming to make a comfortable place for all your kin. Or you may incessantly hoard, never being sure you will ever have enough. Or you may move from one entertainment venue to another, seeking that illusive "it." Or you may fear close interpersonal relationships, so as one turns serious, you may recoil from it, expecting rejection. Or you may fear failure, so you refuse to try something new and different.

As you embrace the "go big" notion, you conquer your fears and insecurities in one sense by being bold and courageous. What often separates you from super-achievers is your ability to face, focus, and fight against anything holding you back, be it personal, physical, or psychological. Most limitations, in my view, are those stemming from how you view yourself.

Some people are driven by *patriotism*, affirming America, for instance, as an exceptional nation. You may forgive all her faults in the name of superiority over other nations. You may prove barracks-brave, calling out foreign enemies, yet you did not enlist in the U.S. military during times of war which might have led to your dying for your lofty ideals. Or you may advocate mean-spirited policies under the guise of "pay your own way" and "personal responsibility" to the point of irreparably rending the social safety net for the less fortunate among us. Or by liberal or progressive leanings, you allow full expression of human depravity to the point that idiocy prevails. Or feeling pulled in opposite directions, you might refuse to take a stand on anything.

Here, "go big" understands that some values are worth fighting for. This spirit, then, fuels informed activism. While you feel inwardly moved, nothing will change in life until you engage: write a letter to the newspaper, e-mail your U.S. representative, e-mail your mayor, draw together like-minded people, vow to end senseless gun violence, defend victims of domestic abuse, teach young women their inherent value, read to children, read the U.S. Constitution, fight for vulnerable children, and more.

Some people are driven by *hedonism*, viewing life as one happy pursuit after another. Here, you might live for the gathering, nightlife, good time, the party, thrills, excitement, and indulgence of every kind associated with pulsating pleasure. You might scale mountains, rappel steep embankments, ride dirt bikes, cliff dive, bungee jump, or fly on skateboards. You'll do anything for the jolt, the high, the adrenaline rush. The riskier the pursuit, the better. Often, this dizzying swirl of events is designed to anesthetize internal pain or to mask the deep frustration of living without essential, ultimate reality. If alcohol, drugs, sex, and violence are added to the mix, just about anything may ensue. The outcome of hedonism is, most often, scary, unsafe, unhealthy, bad, and regrettable.

"Go big" in this regard, at least, seeks to offer a class version of enjoyment. Let me explain: Perhaps attending the symphony, a jazz night, a ballet performance, or touring a museum might be a better expression of wholesome enjoyment. After work or on the weekend, you could dress up and enjoy the ballet with professional colleagues followed by dessert/coffee at a fine dining establishment.

Some people are driven by *life's unrelenting demands*. You might live amid the never-ending hurly-burly, thrust-parry daily grind, and the who's-up, who's-down, what's-new of life. Unfortunately, you never really find peace because your worldview provokes ongoing anxiety. You become angst-ridden, drama-obsessed, nervous, and on edge with a tenuous grasp on the economy, current news, politics, foreign affairs, trends, celebrities, sports, culture, and more. Or you might live with a simple perspective: just make it another day with as little stress and strain as possible. Or you might hide in the anonymity of the crowds of big-city living with all the trappings of success, yet with little joy in your heart.

"Go big" resists yielding to life's tough challenges. Instead, it holds that, like David before Goliath, these existential giants must fall. You must conquer life rather than the other way around! You are infinitely stronger than you may imagine. You have internal reserves that remain untapped. This is your moment, your season, and your time.

Some people are driven by their *ethical center*, viewing life through a prism of moral right and wrong. You might be adamantly opposed to anything against your sense of propriety. You treasure and uphold high spiritual, moral, and ethical standards. Purpose and direction are determined by your core values, inculcated over decades by family, teachers, ethicists, books, and associations.

Intentionally, you give special attention to the proper alignment of your beliefs with concomitant behavioral norms. Not only do you employ godly ethics in your own life, but you also expect others to follow a similar rigorous code of conduct. When you are careful and compassionate, you balance ethics with the challenge of the human struggle for fulfillment. When you are not, your perspective can become haughty, overly critical, and judgmental of others.

When you actualize the "go big" principle, you strive to lead with your morals and ethics, negating any question of your scruples, integrity, or dignity. If you choose to lead others, you must accept scrutiny of your personal character. People will affirm you as uncommon when you demonstrate that uniqueness by a range of means: companions, comportment, conversation, content, and convictions.

Some people are driven by fervor, a spiritual core, or *Christian zeal*. Sincerely, you worship God, serve Him with gladness, and extol the value of Christ as Savior while praying for wisdom, direction, and intimacy with God the heavenly Father. Consistently, you study the Scriptures for timeless principles along with prompts for daily application of such principles to concrete areas of life.

Forthrightly, you aim for integrity, transparency, dignity, decency, and accountability, well aware of a world system which is antithetical to spiritual life in Christ, while being wary of supernatural revelation.

I admire "go big" saints of God because you will expect divine blessings (not always material ones) on the basis of grace. Accordingly, you should thank God profusely, pray incessantly for wisdom, walk cautiously in humility, and seek relentlessly for new converts for His kingdom, while faithfully representing Christ before humanity.

It is hoped that this brief exploration of drive will remind you of the critical significance of its twin, determination. It, too, proves monumental in raising you to the **"Go Big"** level of analysis and achievement.

2) Drive Leads to Determination

"Determination" references possessing a fixed purpose or intention; a necessary agent or factor in reaching a positive outcome; invaluable ingredients for ascertaining an objective; settling on an authoritative or conclusive decision.

Determination fits with all the above regarding drive, in that your drive can only be sustained through your determination. Determination, indeed, propels you through myriad setbacks and moments of despair. Determination reminds you of the importance of your task, the people who will be blessed by it, and the emptiness of the world without it.

On the other hand, let's examine what happens if you are not determined.

3) The Consequences of a Determination Deficit

• When you stopped short of receiving your college degree, even as you are quite intelligent and capable—that was an example of your insufficient determination.

• When you started and failed to complete that major project at work on which depended your evaluation, and possible promotion—that was an example of your determination deficit.

• When you left a troubled marriage because your needs were not met or you were not happy—those were indications of your inability to integrate determination in relational choices. (Marriage is not built on merely meeting personal needs or happiness; rather, it is constructed on God, His grace, faith, love, fidelity, respect, communication, determination, goals, decency, and adventure.)

• When you articulated an intention to purchase a home, started a savings plan for a down payment, yet you are still renting ten years later—that signals your lack of serious determination.

• When you vowed to lose that weight, but twenty pounds kept following you, you were, simply stated, lacking in determination. (In television commercials, Marie Osmond, Jennifer Hudson, and Jessica Simpson make it look so easy!)

- When you promised to give God more of your worship, time, and attention, seeking spiritual grounding in Christ, yet nothing changed—once again, you suffered from a deficit of determination.

- When you walked out of prison after serving your sentence and declared that you would never return, but without job prospects, family ties, or better options, you have returned there—this smacks of a shortage of determination.

- When you repeatedly lose your temper, with excessive anger defining your emotions, spewing vulgarity, invectives, and profanity often at the slightest provocation, while later expressing embarrassment and remorse for such negativity—you evidence a breakdown of determination.

- When you set an important course only to quickly abandon it, yet steadfastly declare your intention to obtain it despite remoteness of the possibility—again you must agree: your determination wavers.

In no way should you become defensive as these issues are raised. While such is tempting, it fails to address the issues raised. Indeed, your defensiveness will defeat your drive and determination. In other words, you can want something but not want it enough. That little word "enough" defines determination.

Fundamentally, you mustn't fault the messenger. Instead, heed the message!

4) Further Descriptions of Determination

If determination could be wrung like a wet towel, it would produce accumulated perspiration. You must want "it" enough to profusely perspire toward its attainment. Championship-caliber athletes never return to the locker room dry, composed, and fresh after a game or match. Instead, they play with abandon, unconcerned with the rivulets of perspiration drenching them and their uniform. Then, after the athletic event they need time to shower, shampoo, apply cologne, and change into street attire. Then we see a better representation of that athlete. As well, note the entertainer. In either case, because they aim for the high achievement they strenuously exert themselves.

That's "go big" in physicality.

Recently, I watched a stage presentation of the classic *The Wizard of Oz*. In the play, viewers are moved as Dorothy, the little girl from Kansas, navigates the journey toward the wizard, along with assorted friends she gathered along the way. I was moved by her determination amid multiple challenges. Over the years, millions have cheered as she faced every imaginable obstacle, first in getting to the wizard, and then in returning home.

That's "go big" in determination.

As I complete this chapter, I am reminded of the ramifications of the "go big" sentiment. An e-mail arrived from an unfamiliar source. In fact, I don't even know how this organization got my e-mail address. Suffice to say, it serves as a great closing. It reads as follows:

> "Next month, I'm turning 67. And more than ever, I want to make an eternal difference with the remaining years of my life.
>
> "I don't want a day to pass where I don't attempt to do at least one thing that will outlive me and last for eternity.
>
> "This year, even after decades of humanitarian ministry, God challenged me to dream bigger than ever before for the future of World Help. Together, with the help of my team and a lot of prayer and careful planning, we created a five-year strategy for what we believe God is leading us to accomplish."

The appeal continues with detailed plans for a visionary venture. World Help seems like a worthwhile mission organization. I am not endorsing them because this represents my initial contact with them. (If you know of them, I encourage you to help them reach this goal. If not, I just gave them free publicity!)

What the e-mail does, however, is illustrate that in attempting any work for God, one must prepare to "go big" with a worldwide focus. If it is for God, the vision/venture must not be narrow, small, provincial, or limited. Thus, I challenge you to dream big!

Should you assess a deficit in drive or in determination, there is still hope. Please consider these relevant facts concerning you.

5) Strategies to Enhance Your Drive and Determination

First, your psychological drive can be enhanced as you surround yourself with overachievers. Literally, when you spend time around those at higher levels than you, their thoughts, behaviors, tastes, and objectives can be discerned. Then, since they have already achieved in a field, emulate what seems useful. Recognize, however, that a copy will never be as sharp as an original. But at least you can aspire to the level of a facsimile. Every day in business, we rely upon faxes to convey grand messages.

Second, as long as you have life and breath, you have infinite opportunities. This world yields to those willing to stand firm for their beliefs (Arab Spring protesters who toppled entrenched dictators; Vietnam protesters who ended an ill-advised war; civil rights protesters who radically changed laws and fostered unprecedented improvements). None can stand against a powerful idea backed by aggrieved, principled, peaceful demonstrators.

Third, each time you are knocked back by adversity, circumstances, emergencies, hurts, pains, losses, and regrets, remember this: every challenge you face and withstand only toughens you for the fight still ahead. However, you are already an achiever because, by the grace of God, you have made it this far!

Fourth, allies come to buoy and buttress you in the midst of your continual striving. No one wants to associate, over a prolonged period, with "sad-sacks," or those prone toward self-pity. Today, I advocate tough love to some who have never taken personal responsibility for their plight. It represents a bitter pill to swallow: you quit school; you married a fool; you joined in with the ignorant crowd; you trusted the wrong person; you gave money to a shyster; you took drugs; you gave your body to the unworthy; you bought the home above your means.

To embellish this tough love philosophy (for those lacking determination), I suggest that parents or spouses pray, converse with the individual, set limits, assess progress, and ask trusted friends to share with you. Then comes the toughest part, having done all these things: give that individual into the hands of God. Mothers and wives will often find this task a difficult one. You will look at your child or mate through rose-colored lens. One kept vow or actual achievement will be magnified. (That's a maternal instinct that men will never fully understand!)

In the end, tough love will aid determination in another because you will refuse many excuses and explanations for failure. At some point, in my judgment, you will have to let someone live with the consequences of his or her choices.

Finally, you must transform volition ("I will") into action ("This is the tangible expression of my declaration.") Otherwise, you will talk incessantly without any discernible evidence of achievement. Somebody must push you and, through this book, I volunteer for the task!

CHAPTER 6

Go Big: Intellect, Intent, and Implementation

Observations of high achievers in America and globally reveal that there are some unusually smart people operating at the top of their field—architects, engineers, scientists, writers, professors, physicians, attorneys, judges, politicians, corporate leaders, entrepreneurs, ministers, artists, and coaches. In too many cases, the rest of us assume that we are locked out of prestige, stature, influence, and material benefits because of our intellectual disadvantage.

Indeed, if you reserve phenomenal achievement to a select few whom you sense as highly intellectual or geniuses, it relieves the majority of humanity from even attempting something internally significant. Yet, I want to probe the matter of intellect, given that you can reach new places of attainment to the degree that you integrate your intellect into a noble, grand, and beneficial objective.

1) Intellect Varies, though It Is Necessary

I raise this "go big" issue, whatever your level of intellect, so that you will join a national and international conversation—among divergent audiences in clubs, groups, associations, fraternities, sororities, union halls, churches, synagogues, barbershops, salons, eateries, and coffee shops—as people assess their ability to transform themselves and the society at-large. I pray that I am reaching many who are already leading the change for progress in the nation and the world. While that sentiment may strike you as an audacious attempt, it is consistent with the overall theme of "go big."

In "go big" theory, thoughts expressed, captured, refined, and honed by stimulating conversations lead to significant breakthroughs with earth-shaking results, often starting in small groups. You may not recognize the potency of simple words, concepts, ideas, and notions. Yet, everything begins with your words, a verbal expression of your intellect. Made in the image of God, you and I have power to create through our words. "The words of a man's mouth are deep waters. . . . Death and life are in the power of the tongue" (Proverbs 18:4a, 21a).

In short, when you speak you charge the atmosphere with thoughts. My Pentecostal friends say it thusly: "I declare and decree it." Though the manifestation may be delayed, what we speak in faith will come to fruition.

When I reference "intellect," it is not, in my view, only doled out in prestigious universities, even those of the Ivy League (Harvard, Yale, Princeton, Stanford, and others) where elitism, money, class, ethnicity, history, ideology, vocabulary, and erudition are assigned the highest values. At the same time, influential colleges help prepare every generation of leaders in various academic disciplines. They also produce professionals in life.

Admittedly, I affirm that many intellectually inclined people in fact didn't attend nor graduate college—any college! But they are unusual, special cases. Most of the rest of us will need to complete our degrees in order to develop professional capacities.

However, many non-college graduates are quite well read and surround themselves with really sharp colleagues, associates, and subordinates. Billionaire Bill Gates of Microsoft fame attended Harvard for one year! Facebook founder Mark Zuckerberg also did not finish college. Yet, they are grand exceptions, fueling technology with "go big" innovative thinking.

Family members with advanced university degrees in the field of education, having studied pedagogical theory, tell me there are multiple intellectual routes. I defer to their superior insight. So, let's further evaluate this notion of intellect.

2) Broad Definitions and Descriptions of *Intellect*

Intellect, as I judge it, represents lifelong acquisition of verifiable knowledge from unbiased sources, open to review and analyses by serious thinkers. Reading, reading, and more reading fuels the intellect. A wide range of books opens vistas to unfamiliar individuals, ideas, ideals, ideologies, and institutions.

Access to other critical thinkers produces a synergy of ideas, with each idea strengthening the validity of another. Once intellect is acquired, accessed, and applied, it must be used for positive purposes. It must never be the focus of arrogance because if you are from any number of minority communities across America, hundreds aided your road to academic success or university achievement.

Intellect involves sound cognitive ability to analyze, evaluate, weigh, appraise, and reach good conclusions from a given set of sources, research, facts, data, and information. You must never consider yourself informed or really intelligent if you accept conclusions from others without exposing such views to the bright light of rigorous examination. No matter how persuasive, you should never blindly embrace another's declaration as truth. Truth is objective, rather than subjective.

Intellect may be sharpened by careful research and time spent in personal study of a topic. In truth, this sharpening involves consultation of reputable sources, tutelage, waiting for more information, sifting through questionable material, asking more questions, and more. A well-honed intellect constantly seeks more knowledge.

Intellect may derive from the Socratic Method: asking a never-ending series of questions with answers leading to subsequent questions. Be careful, however: your incessant questioning of others may expose their fault lines. People would rather have their opinions celebrated than exposed to scrutiny of the validity of their claims. Against this, true intellect rests securely, having obtained a high-quality education honed from spending time in class and in the library, rather than simply traveling across a verdant campus full of bright students. Five- or six-year undergraduate degree programs may allow you to make many friends, but the best students will achieve it in a timely manner.

3) Examples of Rare Intellectual Capabilities

Another manifestation of intellect is creativity to develop a product, a means of producing it, a winning marketing pitch, a mass audience for the product, and a way to get that product to the largest number of interested people. If that formula sounds simple, it's because it was the formula used by Bill Gates of Microsoft fame. Incidentally, by using his intellect (again, one year at Harvard University; he didn't graduate), Gates is now the world's richest man!

Gates and other visionaries (often those undergirding the phenomenal success of Silicon Valley as the incubator of technological innovation) teach the value of innovative intellect and unusual thinking.

Their companies and product offerings are predicated on a "go big" foundation, including companies like Bing, Google, Yahoo, Oracle, Apple, eBay, Amazon, Facebook, Twitter, Instagram, and more.

After a successful product launch, millions ask, "Now, why didn't I think of that?" Each new product line changes the dynamic, with other companies coming along to refine these grand ideas.

Directly related, intellect may be discerned in those called "iconoclastic." That word described the late movie director Robert Altman. He was variously remembered as quirky, offbeat, inventive, a maverick, a misfit, an avatar, and just plain crazy! The reasons for these varied professional characterizations was the entertainment industry's inability to put Altman in a definitive box. Despite unprecedented success with the television comedy *M*A*S*H*, Altman developed an unusual body of work during his long career in motion pictures. Indeed, he was constantly reinventing himself, introducing himself to new audiences over at least two generations.

Altman gave a succeeding generation of filmmakers the vision to "go big" in movie directing. They could experiment with new themes and push the envelope as they offered audiences multiple camera angles, antiauthority protagonists, complex stories, and uncertain endings. In my view, it takes rare intellect to establish an entire genre in filmmaking (films styled similar to his are called "Altmanesque").

In a similar vein, one of my heroes in African-American Christian preaching was the late Dr. A. Louis Patterson Jr. of Houston, Texas. We celebrated a thirty-five-year friendship, even as he was a major ministry mentor to me. Patt was unique in that he charted out fresh territory in preaching. In his messages, one heard a gifted communicator but not, however, in the traditional black Baptist way. He didn't moan, whoop, or have musical timbre in his voice. Instead, his scriptural exegesis, expository insight, vocabulary, illustrations, and connection to human application were rare! Patt was "go big" in the supernatural realm!

Patt popularized alliteration (literary device of two or more adjacent or closely connected words beginning with the same letter or sound) in the preaching art, giving him national standing as a model of the craft. I reiterate his mix of admirable, unique qualities: prayerfulness, integrity, character, thorough exposition of a biblical text, substance, insight, theology, freshness, spirituality, anointing, and an ability to recall difficult concepts with daily application, all centered in Jesus Christ. What an intellect!

Intellect, in another sense, might be tied to an innovative instinct. Persons possessed of the "go big" spirit see opportunity where others are oblivious to it. The ethos of thinking outside the box means processing new ideas through the prism of your cognitive circuitry. This limerick may help: "Think as you've never thought, get what you've never got." Consider the following example.

Jeremy Robbins in Washington, D.C., concerned with the 2014 proposed immigration reform effort making its way through the U.S. Congress, thought to place short ads with his group's perspective in the viewing area behind the front seats of taxicabs there. Every fifteen minutes, these pithy ads ran in 1,300 Washington cabs to the delight or the chagrin of a captive audience of Democrat and Republican legislators, staffers, aides, journalists, pundits, lobbyists, opinion shapers, and others. Note his logic: "That seemed like a way to put an ad where no one else is doing it, and take advantage of all the right eyes being there" (*New York Times,* 7/31/14, p. A15).

Your intellect, finally, may be developed through influence conveyed by ongoing time with a distinguished mentor. (A later chapter is devoted to the value of mentoring relationships.)

By whatever means you acquire intellectual capital, it must be utilized with a high degree of dignity, decency, discipline, and decorum aligning with American sensibilities, principles, logic, reason, and generally accepted mores. In this country and globally, true intellect adheres to the rules of professionalism: punctuality, organization, integrity, negotiation, respect, and customer loyalty.

4) Intellect Connects with Intention

Along with intellect, there must be a sense of intention. The question becomes, "What will you do with this intellect/insight?" In a word, what is your driving intention? What do you really hope to achieve in life?

In its best rendering, your intention clarifies what is most important, rivets you on critical matters, unshackles you from unnecessary obligations, and dismantles outmoded thinking. In the process, it draws new allies to your cause. When intention expresses itself in the "go big" mindset and motif, nothing will long stand in your way!

Your "go big" intention declares to the world, "Look out, I am planning to execute something dynamic and different!"

In the best rendering, your incredible "go big" sentiment coordinates with the credo "When you see the moment, you have to seize the moment." If you want major success, you must recognize that connection along with its demands: hard work, creativity, time, energy, and sacrifice among them.

Most often, the truism holds, "You do what you love, and you do what you do best." Tell me of your passion and, with discipline, I can predict your success or failure rate. Thus, I encourage you to examine your intellect, evaluate your intention, and then move toward accomplishing what you set your heart, mind, and will upon.

Intention relates to the act of determining upon some action, some end, or some conceptualized object. In the movie *Mahogany,* the title song asks, "Do you know where you're going to?"

5) Without Intention, Others Will Define You

Today, if you are unsure of your life intention, leisurely moving with the tide, many will be very happy to escort you. It happens every day as many join a fool's fellowship (those ensnared in poor life choices, embittered, projecting negativity outward). Such people will welcome you to join them in a den of depression—down, depleted, defeated, and dismayed by life. Intellect, however, should link with intention, taking you to a different destination. That different ideology characterizes "go big" people.

Life for you will remain stale, trite, fuzzy, and uncertain as long as intention is missing. Absent intention, you may live amid the accidental, the chance, the haphazard, the inadvertent, the "whatever." If so, you will miss out on what you can bring to fruition by intention.

Even if you sometimes fail, you should always have and faithfully articulate your intention. In a word, if you fail, let it occur while you are attempting great things! Note this comment by one vilified for trying to develop a memorial in Washington, D.C., to

America's thirty-fourth president, Dwight D. Eisenhower: "If I have to walk off the battlefield, it's having given it my best shot." The takeaway: You must always aim high, no matter what!

Athletes and artists down through history gave all their energy on the field or on the stage or screen. Indeed, they were intentional toward success.

Without clarity of intention, you function in a fog amid chaos under cloudy skies where few dreams come to fruition. Without intention, you chase mirages, imagine wells in the desert, and fight invisible enemies.

6) A Sound Equation Involves Intellect, Intention, and Implementation

The "go big" formulation will not allow your intellect and your intention to stop there because it prompts you toward implementation.

"Implementation" refers to putting something into effect according to a procedure. In simple terms, what occupies the mind (intellect and intention) must be put into practice. Often, the matter settles in your mind, getting stuck there and resulting in your inability to bring it to fruition (implementation).

In any substantive objective, implementation is the step that you may miss. And, if missed, you will not discover the full parameters of the "go big" life that is available to you.

Intellect and intention must converse and then converge, with the ultimate objective of implementation.

The idea for completing the novel, graduating college, getting married, opening a savings account, purchasing a home, giving your life to Christ, reading the Bible, praying daily for fifteen minutes, or opening your own business among many endeavors must take a few more steps: intellect plus intention leads to implementation.

In the end, implementation involves a critical process. You may be stymied in a worthy undertaking because you have not thoroughly assessed the full process.

7) Implementation as Definite Action

To write the novel, you must ask yourself some questions: "How shall I begin the novel? Where is my outline? Who are my main characters? What is the driving plot? What conflict will keep readers interested? How do I conclude this effort?"

For the would-be college graduate, you might ask, "How many units am I shy of my degree? Can I obtain a grant, scholarship, financial aid, or some other means of financing my education? Who can I commit this undertaking to to hold me accountable for completing it? What will this degree add to my professional life?"

A prospective bride or groom might ask, "Am I prepared emotionally for a mate? Is this God's will for my life? What will be my responsibilities once I am married? What are my expectations from a mate? After marriage, where will we live? Can I see a realistic future with him/her? What are his/her views of God? Faith? Children? Goals? Money? Can we grow together? Can we laugh together? What will life be like when we are older?"

Even coming to God, you should ask some questions: "Is my life now full of peace, hope, and purpose? What if Christ really is the way to God? What might happen if I pray? Could worship be the key to my fulfillment? Are there benefits of Bible study? What is this 'spiritual life' all about?"

The business owner should engage in this same process: "Is my business plan stated in such a way that someone will invest with me? Can I remain in business if this idea takes three months to explode? How much am I willing to sacrifice for the success of my dream? Are there similar businesses in my immediate area? What is my marketing strategy? Marketing budget? Community demographics?

Again, let me repeat: if your objective (personal, psychological, professional) is a worthy one, you should take the time to move through the full process. Start with the intellect, move to the intention, and end with the implementation.

Recently, I was in a Target store. I went in for a few items. While browsing, I thought of other items I needed. After twenty minutes of shopping, regrettably, I had more items than I had originally come in for. At the checkout counter, everything culminated. There, implementation was realized. As long as I wandered down aisles, there was not a challenge. (Life allows continual browsing.) With a credit card, I was able to implement, to accomplish what I set out to do (only with more items!), which was bring home necessary goods for our family.

Every day, you have multiple opportunities for implementing your dreams. There will never be a better day than today to harness your intellect and your intention as you expect the "it" to occur. The key to implementation is being willing to risk failure, humiliation, the wrong answer, or the denial of a request. Conversely, implementation may result in success, applause, the correct answer, or the approval of your request.

8) Never Stop Short of Implementation

At its foundation, implementation refuses to remain idle while so much occurs around you. Or, implementation recognizes that if you procrastinate too long, wonderful privileges will pass you by. Or, implementation reasons that right now is just as good a time as later for making your profound impact.

If the Wright brothers had simply thought of the possibilities of aircraft without implementation of their aeronautic theories, you couldn't today board a jet plane bound for London, Madrid, or Paris.

If Ray Croc had settled for conceptualizing rather than actually opening a fast-food stand, you couldn't today obtain a burger, fries, and drink at thousands of McDonald's stores worldwide.

If Henry Ford had accepted the innumerable challenges of building a motor vehicle, choosing to dream only without building both cars and assembly lines, you couldn't today drive hundreds of miles toward your destination.

9) Sharpening Your Intellect, Intent, and Implementation

First, in order to enhance your intellectual capital you must read widely; or surf the Internet; or enroll in classes; or join with a mentor; or some combination thereof. The body of knowledge upon which you base decisions must constantly expand. The twenty-first-century world revolves on empirical data and verifiable metrics, a world where competence and analytical rigor rule. That world admires an unsentimental, pragmatic, real-life approach. Accordingly, you must not totally rely upon instinct, hunches, suppositions, superstitions, rumors, or speculations. If you don't know, you can find the answer relatively easily and quickly.

Second, if you clearly state your intent, others will be prone to follow your lead. Of course, in the transmission of your intent you may have to repeat more slowly what you initially stated. For me, I am really moved and motivated by written presentations of leaders or change agents. In that way, your message is less prone to get confused.

Indeed, I am both aware and mystified by the aversion some leaders have toward the written vision of their objectives. On one hand, I wonder if they are incapable of written expression. On the other hand, I wonder if the matter has to do with willful attempts to confuse, allowing people to form their own judgments rather than making clear, definitive goals plain for all to see and verify.

Third, so much of what you aim to achieve will fail in its implementation stage. You start with a great idea. It has some practical benefit. You start toward its attainment. In this process, you refine your goals with additional data. Ultimately, you figure out everything except how to actually make it work. You factor in everything except what may spoil the entire project. And what you fail to adequately think through ends up dooming the entire venture. The problem involves implementation. The poet Robert Burns famously lamented, "The best laid plans o' mice and men often go awry."

Fourth, you increase the likelihood of achievement by the degree to which you are willing to monitor the process as it winds its way to implementation. Here is an example of what I mean: Public utilities, schools, and companies, even when you leave all the pertinent callback information on the voicemail or in the e-mail, may not return your call or e-mail. Though these entities should, they do not always register high, in my view, in customer service. To deal with this, I suggest you call them until you get satisfaction. You do this with insistence in a firm, professional manner without vulgarity or rudeness. If a week passes without resolution, call them again!

Indeed, you cannot leave anything of importance to the whims of others, be they colleagues or subordinates. People, in many cases, sincerely endeavor to work on your project; but they prioritize their own.

If by some stretch of imagination others think of advancing your work, they may—may!—think of you. As you consider your project critical, you must keep it on the minds of those who may be inclined to assist you. In the Bible, Joseph makes a plea to a prison mate: "Only keep me in mind when it goes well with you, and please do me a kindness by remembering me to Pharaoh, and get me out of this house" (Genesis 40:14). I wish that the Bible were silent on the outcome, but it records the bitter truth: "Yet the chief cupbearer did not remember Joseph, but forgot him" (Genesis 40:23). Sadly, today there are millions of cupbearers alive in the world!

Finally, you achieve "go big" because in this sense, you recognize the nexus of intellect, intention, and implementation. Often, you may not see them as three separate threads, but rather as one seamless garment. If the garment called successful attainment fits you well, then no matter. Indeed, success looks good on you! Wear it in grace and gratitude to God.

Chapter 7

Go Big: Values and Vision

As we plunge deeper into the nature of phenomenal personal achievement, the "go big" model, you must acknowledge the importance of values and vision, separating one from the other. While some strive for great things, others settle for mediocrity. Some relish the privileges of a famous last name while ignoring its responsibilities. Others enjoy simply sharing the air and atmosphere of achievers. Unfortunately, some have little or no ambition for achievement. What explains these divergent outlooks? Much of the achievement difference may stem from fundamentally different internal values.

1) Values Help You Visualize Life

Values undergird visions of what is available in your life, the parameters of what you consider possible, and how to reach new levels of attainment. In a real sense, then, values fuel your vision toward something noble, monumental, lasting, and enduring.

From early in life until your death, you are a collection of values: core principles, ideas, and ideals around which life is organized. In short, values represent what you live by. The accumulation of values produces your ideology and driving philosophy.

In the initial sense, values are taught, usually conveyed by your parents or your family of origin. Your parents or grandparents may have constantly emphasized core concepts for a meaningful existence:

1. "Love God always."
2. "Love people."
3. "Help the needy."
4. "Respect yourself and others."
5. "Work hard."
6. "Save your money."
7. "Finish the task."

8. "Be true to your word."

9. "Watch the company you keep."

10. "Aside from God, don't trust anyone for all your needs."

11. "Take your time, but get it done."

12. "In life, you will have many associates but only a few true friends."

These admonitions underscore core values. Simple and succinct, they capture something fundamental in you. Decades after hearing the words uttered, you still relish the depth of their inherent value.

Young children, teens, and every adolescent should hear, and hopefully heed, the values of their parents. The parents' hope involves a successful transmission of values, so as to perpetuate maturity, independence, healthy self image, life skills, beneficial habits, socialization, problem solving, and wise decision making, amid competing value systems.

In the absence of parents' transmitting values to impressionable children and youth, we sorely need cherished institutions (churches, schools, service clubs, mentors, community groups, and government) to fill that void.

At some point, notwithstanding values passed from older generations, you must personally evaluate and commit to a moral, ethical, spiritual, political, economic, personal, existential, and pragmatic perspective. In a word, you must determine what you hold dear—what you consider as ultimate truth—which will then determine the trajectory of your ambitions.

Parents and adults, concerned about future generations, must pointedly and prominently express their value system. Its espousal will create a culture of expectations for those given to your care.

Let's consider these value foundations:

2) Range of Values

Biblical values emanate from respecting, reading, believing, meditating upon, and adhering to the Bible while celebrating its timely and timeless principles.

Currently, some wish to argue that the Holy Bible represents nominally a good book, focusing on its familiar themes (love, goodness, kindness, hospitality) rather than affirming it as clear revelation from God—inspired, inerrant, infallible, authoritative—designed to guide individuals in honoring God and in embracing salvation through Jesus Christ while living in harmony with the divine will.

You represent a fundamental shaper and molder of biblical values for your progeny and other impressionable youth. Further, you are charged by God with directing youth along a particular path. When you articulate the Holy Bible as the singular repository of absolute truth for humanity with Christ the Son of God as its apex, you immeasurably develop younger persons as accountable to their Creator.

At the same time, when you converse with younger persons with the Bible as the foundation for guidance, you prepare them for a world that rejects the reality of absolutes. In my view, morals and ethics must be based on an objective standard. In light of God's grace toward humanity, unchanging principles, and a well-established order of the universe, you take solace in His care of all details of human existence.

Since all persons operate by some code of conduct, some value system, it behooves you to examine your ultimate motivation. Then, share that value system with those whom you love. It is a dangerous proposition, in my judgment, when mature adults leave their children, grandchildren, and other youth to the vagaries of a value-free, morally neutral worldview. Instead, parents must clearly articulate the organizing principles of their lives. Failing to do so, in my view, constitutes moral child abuse.

Eroding biblical values in America expose your children and youth to a kaleidoscope of ideologies, notions, and concepts, ones often antithetical to the Judeo-Christian biblical worldview. Tragically, faced with such assaults youth accept any well-presented, innocuous-sounding theory as the font of their life outlook. Increasingly, militant assaults on biblical mores are led by secular college professors, liberal media, corporate leaders, "politically correct" pundits, liberal churches/ministers, and others. The totality of these assaults rends the moral fabric carefully woven over the centuries by strong biblical principles.

Let me be clear: the Holy Bible truly matters in determining values!

In the larger scheme, you create and cultivate a culture of "go big" as you stand boldly on the Word of God as the ultimate organizing principle for a meaningful life, while intentionally transmitting such principles to others. I admonish you with this: seize this moment by sharing your biblical values with your children, other youth, and all others with whom God has given you influence. In so doing, you will immeasurably equip them for successful navigation of life's challenges.

3) Moral Values

In the main, *moral values* represent objective principles of right and wrong which underpin life. These principles should guide the behaviors, choices, associations, and outlooks of those seeking to operate from a moral perspective. Armed with a moral compass operative over a lifetime, individuals will live according to principle rather than the necessity of the moment.

Moral values are not contingent on circumstances, as principles involve normative, non-negotiable truth, from which the conscience will not deviate. Indeed, if you are of high moral values, you'd rather lose friendships than to submit to ideas and ideologies which go against your entrenched and embedded principles.

Equally important, norms of right and wrong initially emerge from parents' teaching (or lack thereof). Later, you learn to process external stimuli (from teachers, books, television, radio, internet, wider culture, friends, classmates, and the like) as critical value determinants. In some way, you are a product of unlimited inputs by others, through various encounters.

Most wise, moral, godly parents hope children (teenagers, mainly) will have embraced their values when those teenagers are formulating their goals and dreams in life. As Christians, you and I have a vested interest in seeing these values displayed through a life of stellar accomplishment, honoring God, and exemplifying Christ while blessing others. Today, amid external negatives polluting American culture, if you succeed in inculcating such values in your progeny, consider yourself a really successful parent.

Early in the twenty-first century, we hear that the younger demographic (Millennials) have little regard for what some term rigid moral and social values of previous generations. It is arguable that moral and ethical standards have been lowered or compromised by the present generation of young people. What is indisputable, however, is that many adults shy away from expressing their sense of acceptable behavior for those still searching for answers.

This inability or unwillingness on the part of parents to share guiding moral values leads to an absence of such values in teens, youth, and young adults. The multifaceted thug culture in urban America (obscenity, drugs, sagging pants, piercings, tattoos, hats turned sideways, materialism, coarseness, violence, sexual objectification of women, hedonism, children sired without responsible fathers, buffoonery, and so on) illustrates moral and ethical confusion. Low moral standards manifest themselves in cases of both "I don't know" (ignorance) and "I don't want to know" (pride). That, in my view, is a damning combination!

The lack of a substantive moral foundation results in a world characterized by the poet Langston Hughes's ominous question from 1951: "What happens to a dream deferred?" Conversely, today many American youth might ask, in the words of *New York Times* columnist Charles M. Blow, "What happens when one desists from dreaming, when the very exercise feels futile?"

So as American youth culture steadily deteriorates, I am really concerned. As an antidote, I challenge Christian parents and those equally concerned to earnestly inculcate moral values among impressionable youth. If you do not, this sensate, secular culture will gladly provide youth with an ungodly worldview. The current worldview is called "post-modernism," and the youth and young adults of this generation live without moral absolutes. Its manifestations are lack of respect for authority figures, normalization of alcohol and drug use, promiscuity, laziness, indifference or ambivalence toward the future, devaluing of institutions, lack of historical perspective, and more.

The issue is, will loving parents share their life principles, or will they allow the dominant culture to dictate mores? While it proves easy to blame youth for a lack of morals, it is far more complex to connect such conditions with the failure of moral adults to convey those principles.

Part of what disturbs me regarding moral values is the steady declining role of institutions—family, school, church, government—in shaping larger cultural norms. America's so-called leaders encourage a value-free world as the best option for all. They espouse free expression—personally, relationally, sexually, and morally—so long as "you don't hurt others." Further, their guiding philosophy declares, "You must be true to yourself." In my mind, that liberal ideology was forever debunked in 1960s America.

Fifty years of insolence among youth and young adults has generated seeds of rebellion, unrest, strife, and questioning of moral precepts. The current crop is now an American society given to misplaced principles. Even the response to police shootings of unarmed black men in America—"Black Lives Matter," for instance—in many cases, represents protest without a program. Such will never produce legislation, new training protocols, or fundamental reforms.

In that spirit, I encourage you to seek to inspire succeeding generations to embrace the "go big" construct as a moral imperative. You can convince them of the old notion that each generation goes further than the previous one.

4) Political Values

In national politics, you'd not be surprised that some prominent families are Democrat (Kennedys, Carters, Clintons), while others are staunchly Republican (Bushes, Cheneys, Romneys). This reality is not accidental. Instead, within the family culture, animating *political values* (public service, changing the world, raising concerns, fighting for justice, small government, or a strong military) lead generations to a shared political conclusion. In so many ways, these families (and their web of former aides, staffers, friendships, lobbyists, pundits, and donors) drive the national conversation regarding political values (lower taxes, immigration reform, foreign aid, education, jobs, voting, and more). Further, these values foster new public policy initiatives.

Most Americans will never exert the kind of influence as the families referenced above, perhaps due to those families' social status, fame, notoriety, offices held over the last five or six decades, extensive ties to donors, or economic clout. When all of these benefits combine, it is little wonder that the political field (presidential, federal, and state levels) has been dominated by just a few well-known families. Correctly, we assert that their values have made politics the "family business" in America.

Unwittingly or deliberately, then, you pass political values on to your children: America rewards those with a solid, quality education, who will work hard and play within the rules while expecting equal opportunities. Or you may convey the notion of a colorblind, egalitarian, post-racial country with opportunities aplenty for all who pursue them. Or you may pass on cynicism to the next generation: America leans toward the connected, those of a certain race, or socioeconomic status, and no matter what, systemic racism will inevitably demonstrate itself.

In evaluation of this matter, political values fuel a "go big" sentiment to the degree that members of beloved political families start their political careers with a built-in advantage (name recognition, funding, staffing, and polling) over lesser-known, equally qualified opponents.

For any person, the "go big" emphasis means that your political values will fuel being registered to vote and voting as a cornerstone of democracy and a bedrock principle of responsible engagement in civic affairs. Further, if you are so inclined, your political values may mean putting yourself forward for an elected position, especially when there are issues about which you are passionate.

In this regard, no ethnic, racial, or religious entity should ever so align itself unquestioningly with either political party. The Democratic and Republican parties both represent important political values. Neither party should be demonized by its opponents nor lionized by its adherents. Instead of permanent alliances, you should give your vote to the candidate or platform which best exemplifies your personal political values. From one election to another, the platform or candidate may change, but your value system should remain constant.

5) Economic Values

In America, from birth onward individuals are shaped by the free enterprise, free market, capitalistic system. Theorist and economist Adam Smith offers the foundational tenets of capitalism. It also serves as the infrastructure of *economic values*. Implicitly, you and I accept its central tenets. You share its essential presuppositions (education, expertise, experience, creativity, ideas, productivity, inheritance, work, savings, and investments) as well as its outcomes (personal income, dividends, interest, wealth, taxation, return-on-investment, private ownership, freedom from governmental interference, and so forth).

People from other countries envy the American economic system because it affords those who dedicate themselves to developing a product, providing a service, or conceiving a great idea the benefits of their labor, time, energy, and creativity. In the process, that person may start with little or nothing in the way of material benefits, yet within, say, ten years, the same person may own a home and/or business while enjoying the security of a pension along with other accoutrements of the American dream!

This economic value system, as I see it, should be shared with more youth, particularly African-American ones. You must not assume young people will learn the value of a dollar, celebrate a work ethic, understand the importance of saving, relish the wisdom of investments, or embrace the necessity of deferred gratification while practicing fiscal discipline and many other sound principles without your active input.

Young men and women of Silicon Valley fame, those who embody the "go big" philosophy in technology, were given the freedom to dream, often by successful parents or strong mentors. You can foster those same attainment traits if you deliberately aim to positively impact the next generation.

I encourage you to celebrate the skill sets of young urban minorities (negotiation, quick wit, charisma, supply-demand dynamics, relationship building, problem solving, "hustling," and others) as the foundation for success in life. Some street skills will prove beneficial in other disciplines, whether enrolling in college, enlisting in the armed forces, or applying for employment.

While America has made considerable progress in race relations in my own lifetime (since the early 1960s), including electing a black president in 2008 and reelecting him in 2012, our country has not made nearly enough progress in elevating the lives of most young men of color. Black youth are not animals to be feared by whites; young African Americans will often make mistakes in judgment, just as white youth will. That's why police reform must start with sensitivity training of officers who often encounter minority youth who emerge from a totally different cultural milieu.

If they are properly educated, acculturated, and assimilated into the American economic mainstream, black youth will sense a stake in possessing and preserving the American dream: freedom, dignity, respect, decency, gainful employment, owning property, and saving for the future while providing for their families and children.

For example, the February 2014 $200 million My Brother's Keeper five-year initiative by the Obama administration sought to intentionally improve the plight of black and Latino youth, especially boys. Increasingly, it has been shown that they are lacking in skills, employment, role models, and other necessary ingredients for a successful future. When more African-American youth are still more likely to end up in jail or languish in the criminal justice system than they are in a job or in college, we see the depth of the situation. Accordingly, we should celebrate such programs and more as significant ways to ensure brighter futures for at-risk youth populations.

My prayer involves those with economic incentives summoning the "go big" impulse, as you comprehend the role economic values play leading to a lifetime of success, fulfillment, and provision for yourself and your family. In no way should financial security as an economic objective be viewed as greed or materialism. Rather, it is vital that you appreciate the American economic model of capitalism as a viable alternative to moving forward in life. When achievement brings an economic advantage it fuels drive, focus, and creativity.

6) Artistic and Athletic Values

Music, dance, literature, painting, and the plethora of athletics (soccer, baseball, football, basketball, field hockey, lacrosse, golf, swimming, volleyball, tennis, and others) represent a range of activities that can be shaped by values. The former represents a range of *artistic and athletic values.*

Many well-meaning parents lay before their children a menu of interests and activities from which the child or youth may choose to participate. In so many ways, parents are intentionally directing children or youth in healthy directions. After youth complete the regular school day, parents are expected to enroll their children and encourage healthy pursuits during early evenings and weekends so that children will be "well-rounded." Important skills and life lessons are shared in organized activities with other children and youth. Participating in these interests and activities form the rubric of basic socialization.

While I celebrate this parental value conveyance, I would add a note of caution: Do not aim to resolve issues from your own past by steering your children in a particular direction. For example, if you aspired to shine as a cheerleader back in high school but was not chosen for the squad, it is not fair to insist that your daughter follow in that path. She may or may not have the skill set for a similar pursuit. The same applies for the failed musician never invited to perform with the school band. Your child, again, may not possess the required discipline and coordination for that engagement.

I assert that while values may be espoused (art is aesthetically profound; dance opens worlds of creativity; athletics enshrine teamwork, sportsmanship, and patience; music resonates deep in the human spirit; reading transports to new realms of insight; chess enhances analytical thinking), talent, giftedness, drive, and certain abilities represent something deeper. Someone has said, "You can't teach talent."

By temperament, I am a reader. Allow me to read novels, memoirs, biographies, newspapers, magazines, journals, and Bible commentaries, and I am blissfully complete. My two children, however, are part of the frenetic, technological, short-attention-span, social-media generation. For them, reading is fundamentally quite boring!

My son, my namesake, Jarvis II, played varsity basketball in high school. I was and am immensely proud of his sports successes. Even today, he remains passionate regarding basketball. More importantly, in May 2015 he received a Bachelor's degree in Communications from Howard University in Washington, D.C. Inherently a quiet young man, his maternal grandmother often remarks, "Jarvis II just won't talk!"

My daughter, my "twin," Jillian, still relatively young, absolutely loves the fine arts of dance (tap, ballet, jazz, contemporary, hip-hop) and gymnastics. Again, more important to me, I pray she does well in essential academic areas (math, reading, science, history, social studies). I am already speaking of her attending Harvard University!

So, my value on handling the printed word (the reflection of research, meditation, preparation, discussion, critique, and more) has not been successfully conveyed or embraced by my own progeny. I am sure they cannot fully appreciate my passion for reading, while I abhor their attachment to technological devices. In my estimation, such devices stymie face-to-face human interaction and meaningful conversation.

7) Personal Values

Despite the best intentions of parents, teachers, mentors, counselors, pastors, and others, you must individually embrace some value system if you seek a life of substance, dignity, engagement, and achievement. Ask yourself, What are my *personal values?*

I am well aware of very successful parents across multiple disciplines whose biological children are abject failures at just about any endeavor to which they set themselves. Indeed, educators don't always produce children fond of learning. Tycoons don't always produce offspring respectful of business success. Entertainers don't always produce children who can carry a tune. And Christian ministers don't always produce children who love, honor, and revere God. As well, history, literature, and current culture bear out the fact that none can draw a direct line from stellar parents to equally stellar children, in terms of life achievement.

8) Family Values

The whole point of this chapter is to demonstrate the source of values, especially those which constitute the emotional infrastructure of the "go big" spirit in individuals. Notwithstanding acclaimed geniuses, most achievers emerge from the communication of family values. Along with those expressed much earlier, family values include respect for education, spirituality in Christ, family solidarity, ability to elucidate your views, hands-on good works, supporting the less-fortunate, and more.

Let me polish this point. It is quite possible to live in the home of, serve under the influence of, and walk in the footsteps of tremendously successful figures without reaching similar heights. Simply occupying the orbit of a great father, a loving and supportive mother, an achieving mentor, a phenomenal teacher, a compassionate pastor, or some other person of accomplishment will not mean the same success for the next generation.

What often goes wrong in values transmission?

9) Values Are Conveyed by Intentional Acts

Part of the answer may be that persons of earlier generations were tied to a deep, abiding value system—one that secured their attainment despite setbacks, abuse, racism, bigotry, obstacles, and other impediments to success. No matter what came against these exceptional leaders, they were sustained by deeply ingrained values. Resolutely, they committed to God, to themselves, and to others: "I will not flinch, nor fall back, nor fail, no matter what!"

In the toughest of times, people of embedded values rise to meet the challenges set before them. You can take a page from the book of the late Dr. Robert Schuller of Crystal Cathedral fame. He popularized the saying "Tough times don't last, but tough people do."

The key to producing tough-minded children is to lovingly explain the nuances of life, a life that is full of choices and consequences. Though you love them deeply and dearly, you cannot always be their safety net (financial or otherwise). You must allow them to fail, all while under your constant watchfulness. Then, children must learn from their mistakes so as to avoid the same poor choices in the future. When they get up and try again by their own decision, volition, and actions, you will have succeeded as a parent.

10) Deeply Embedded Values Last a Lifetime

Again, I must emphasize a central truth of this chapter. From whatever source, all live by their values (intentionally or inadvertently). In fact, when you lose material possessions, acclaim, fame, or the features of success, your true character is defined by the values to which you have committed your life.

Moreover, even when you are incapable of fully articulating your values or the means by which you arrived at them, you still live out your embedded values. Good parents or poor ones, engaged or absent parents, caring or negligent teachers, wise or inane mentors, patient or insensitive pastors—they assist in the formation and transmission of values.

This extended discussion of multiple values should underscore the fact that those who possess the "go big" mentality have adopted certain core values. These values help shape and mold life. These values lead to your success or failure. These values direct dreams, analyses, behaviors, associations, outlook, perspectives, and expectations.

In the ongoing debate as to whether leaders are born or developed, I understand the side that champions those with inherent qualities, seemingly from birth, positioning them for stellar leadership positions. Yet, most in that camp would agree that latent leadership tendencies must be honed and sharpened over time by sharp, sensitive, caring mentors so that all that is within you will be manifest, bringing leadership to its fullest fruition.

In short, those who will continually exhibit the "go big" spirit are those with the inclination for unusual leadership as well as having a deeply embedded value system.

11) Who Are You? (A Values Question)

If you are stripped of titles, external benefits, applause, and fame, you still have enough to start life anew if you retain your core values. In fact, if you view it correctly, achievement represents the culmination of inherent values coming to the surface. The old saying holds true: "Cream rises to the top."

Along with core internal values, the "go big" theme is confirmed by vision. Again, to build our thesis we start with definitions of the terms involved.

12) Vision Must Be Defined

Vision captures the capacity for unusual foresight; an imaginative conception or anticipation; an image or idea seen in the mind's eye.

Vision proves beneficial to the degree it escapes the cognitive circuitry of one's mind, representing his/her conceptual capabilities. Great, compelling, deep thoughts must be written, developed, and nurtured while being augmented by advisers, colleagues, friends, research, and the lapse of time. Indeed, you do not really think in your brain, but on paper. The rough draft of articulated thought represents the starting point for tremendous insight.

Effective leaders across diverse fields, not surprisingly, are endowed with several traits, among them being vision—seeing beforehand the needs of those they seek to serve. Once leaders articulate their sense of direction for an entity, they must passionately pursue it for the benefit of all the people involved. Various words and phrases describe this phenomenon: teamwork; organizational efficiency; and optimal institutional functionality, for example. United achievement, then, is sweetened as leader and people arrive at a preferred objective.

In the "go big" formulation, those with vision (visionaries) most often see themselves in a place long before its actual onset. Prior to full realization, visionaries envision completing college, going to the military, owning a business, getting married, having children, holding steady employment, writing a novel, owning a home, enjoying a professional promotion, composing a symphony, or some other achievement. They find supreme joy in moving from concept to fruition.

Further, "vision" references an image coming to you through divine or supernatural assistance. God's calling to Christian ministry as a lifelong vocation falls in the area of vision. Clearly, what God placed in my spirit regarding sharing Jesus Christ with humanity in June 1978 could not be fully articulated then, nor can it fully explain, even now, what has sustained my focus—Christian ministry—over nearly forty years' duration.

13) Obtaining and Developing Your Vision

This chapter inextricably joins together *values* and *vision*. In some way, those with an undergirding value system with an arc bent toward "go big" will discover some internal character traits propelling them forward. Elsewhere in this book, I have tried to explain it: Your values cause you to expect unusual accomplishments in and for your life. This feeling is not arrogance, nor is it reflective of a sense of entitlement. To celebrate self-worth does not mean others lack worth or significance.

How, then, do you cultivate values and vision?

First, you should thoroughly examine your values and their source. Once you truly know yourself (values), you then extrapolate as to what constitutes commensurate achievement. In other words, you chart your outcome from the accumulation of inputs. Since I abhor the notions of luck, "right place, right time," cards dealt, happenstance, "ship coming in," or anything suggesting the absence of the hand of God in human lives, I enjoy discussion of God's grace, mercy, and love.

The vision you develop of yourself and of others emerges from your value system. If you have a negative self-image, it can change as you better evaluate yourself as a person in the present rather than a product of the past. I am truly nauseated by all those who cite early challenges (father left the home, abuse by a relative, poverty cycle, lack of education, blighted communities, narrow vistas, lack of mentors, racism, unfair policies, negative people, bullying, and so on). I wish I knew a better way of saying it, but, "So what! Now, get over it!"

Millions have faced and conquered similar situations. That personal responsibility and tough love sensibility will help you succeed. And when you affirm Jesus Christ as Savior, He brings you into the dimension of the inexplicably "new" (see 2 Corinthians 5:17). There, your attitude, aspirations, associations, and altitude change!

The turning point for young achievers in many cases down through history has been the compassionate involvement of engaged figures: parents, teachers, coaches, or mentors. Yet, fundamentally, true change requires supernatural intervention by God, resulting in spiritual and moral transformation. And the basis of that change is truly a dynamic relationship with God through His Son, Jesus Christ.

Second, as you embrace a spiritual transformation centered in Christ you will be renewed, recharged, reanimated, and reoriented for higher purposes. New life in Christ is far better than a rebuilt engine; indeed, it involves a brand-new one. Now, redeemed by faith in Christ, you love God, love yourself, and love humanity. The Bible validates this new ethic: "And He said to them, 'You shall love the Lord your

God with all your heart, and with all your soul, and with all your mind'" (Matthew 22:37).

Third, you must enjoy a vision of your better life to which you are required to contribute your mind, emotion, and will. Christian, biblical theologians speak of an individual's *trichotomous* (three-part: intellect, emotion, and will) nature. Just as earthly entities such as corporations, schools, and the like spend time developing vision statements, I advise that you do the same. Ask this question: "With my inculcated values, what vision do I have of myself?"

Fourth, you enhance values, leading to a greater vision, when you realize that you have rights to fulfillment, purpose, marriage, employment, happiness, material prosperity, intelligence, health, respect from and good treatment by others, industriousness, and more. These rights should not be confused with the litany of rights given in America's founding documents. Rather, these are inherent rights granted by God, sanctioned by Christ, and developed by self-examination.

Finally, you embrace vision to the degree that you want and work toward all that God has ordained for you. Though achieving a large vision will not be easy, the time, energy, and effort involved and the rush attained from it will prove worthy of all that was expended!

CHAPTER 8

Go Big: Time Management

Very early in the Introduction, we noted that everyone potentially can embrace this "go big" ethos because we all operate within a 24-hour day, 7-day week, 365-day year, divided into 12 months. If you add the four seasons of a year, you determine unlimited possibilities. Indeed, time represents the common factor linking you to the rest of humanity. No one gets more time than another. And no one gets less of it than another. In fact, the key is wise utilization of your time, manifesting passion, creativity, and ingenuity.

Scripture has a great deal to convey regarding time: "There is an appointed time for everything. And there is a time for every event under heaven" (Ecclesiastes 3:1). Or, "Whatever your hand finds to do, do *it* with *all* your might; for there is no activity or planning or knowledge or wisdom in Sheol where you are going. . . . Moreover, man does not know his time: like fish caught in a treacherous net and birds trapped in a snare, so the sons of men are ensnared at an evil time when it suddenly falls on them" (Ecclesiastes 9:10, 12).

At the same time, we may consider other biblical references to time, beginning with Hosea 10:12: "Reap in accordance with kindness; Break up your fallow ground, For it is time to seek the LORD Until He comes to rain righteousness on you." Or, "But be sure of this, that if the head of the house had known at what time of the night the thief was coming, he would have been on the alert and would not have allowed his house to be broken into" (Matthew 24:43). Or, "And He said, 'Go into the city to a certain man, and say to him, "The Teacher says, 'My time is near; I *am* to keep the Passover at your house with My disciples'"'" (Matthew 26:18). Or, "But this I say, brethren, the time has been shortened . . ." (1 Corinthians 7:29a).

Further, we might benefit from other biblical admonitions: "Let us not lose heart in doing good, for in due time we shall reap if we do not grow weary" (Galatians 6:9). Or, "Blessed is he who reads and those who hear the words of the prophecy, and heed the things which are written in it; for the time is near" (Revelation 1:3).

In my view, the cumulative weight of Scripture, then, teaches wise evaluation of and prompt engagement in time as it is a precious gift from our Creator. How a Christian utilizes time speaks to that believer's analysis of God as well as his or her sense of purpose, aspiration, achievement, and personal fulfillment in the name of Jesus Christ.

Yet, to a large extent, you will be stymied in your pursuit of unusual accomplishment, not because of the evil of others but because you did not properly apply yourself within the framework of allotted time. In fact, through a variety of ways you can waste much time only to discover that time represents a commodity that you can't retrieve once it is lost.

Mere busy-ness amid a hurried, hectic, hurly-burly schedule must never serve as a substitute for conscientious usage of time. Often, in "running around" you may run into yourself! Yet, you will not make sustained progress.

Once, a Christian colleague inquired of me as a busy, dutiful, involved, socially minded pastor: "Collier, as a busy pastor, when and where do you find time to also write books?"

Upon reflection, his question had merit, even as I had not spent much time processing it. Perhaps I simply worked it all into my full schedule. Yet, the short answer as to where one "finds" time for multiple projects is this: you must give priority to the things that are priorities; everything else must wait!

In taking care of a local Christian congregation with many people vying for my attention, I must budget my time every day: early morning prayer/reflection; home chores; arrival at the office; conversing with the staff; visiting the sick; presiding over memorials; studying for sermons/Bible studies; and more. As with spending money, the lack of a budget produces frustration. Similarly, a busy pastor must give time to all that constitutes his/her responsibilities before God.

As writing books represents part of my calling and assignment from God, I strive to allocate three hours uninterrupted each day for reading, organizing thoughts, writing, and polishing several book concepts. This period occurs usually in the afternoon just prior to any evening ministry meeting or engagement I must attend.

Often, as community meetings occur I must send my regrets because, in my judgment, I can either attend everything or concentrate on those matters which will constitute a legacy of achievement. So while I pastor a vibrant congregation, I am also developing as a Christian writer, while pursuing a grocer for our neglected urban community.

To answer the brother's question as to when I find time to write, let me state my time-management philosophy. Daily, I find it refreshing that I keep my appointment with my computer, composing thoughts, generating outlines, reading, revising, and considering the finished product. Check that: I am almost never satisfied with the product. In fact, if left to my own devices, I would write a book, critique it, and then write a new one in its place! My own inclination to finish what I start—and wise editors—keeps me on schedule.

Moreover, with the priest and prophetic mantle, in our community I advocate for more sensitive policing, greater employment opportunities for black youth, affordable housing, healthcare for all; yet, I am incomplete.

Fundamentally, I give my full attention to my family as well. Time at home, conversations, laughter, prayer, television, movies, dance recitals, dinners, and outings constitute the vibrancy of our time together. In the end, the family dynamic influences more lives over a longer period of time, thus ensuring a personal legacy.

Moreover, in some weird world, I am acutely aware of nationally acclaimed pastors/authors whose ministries are far larger than my own; yet, they generate scores of books. In this listing, I would place Charles Stanley, Chuck Swindoll, Max Lucado, Rick Warren, Tony Evans, Kenneth Ulmer, Joel Osteen, T. D. Jakes, Donald Hilliard, DeForest "Buster" Soaries Jr., H. B. Charles Jr., and others. Please do not read that I harbor envy or jealousy of their writing gifts, as all must bring glory to God. Indeed, if you aspire to grow you must conceptualize your comrades!

I am possessed by the opinion that if God can use these Gospel giants in explaining the Word in writing and in speaking, while serving in a local Christian ministry setting (pastorate), why couldn't God use me as well?

What specific principles can we ascertain from this discussion of time?

1) Time Is Neutral

You fill your time with, you spend your days on, matters you deem as important, while others are less so. You must determine what you will prioritize. Family dynamics, television, news, dramas, athletics, or entertainment can consume your twenty-four-hour day, preventing remarkable achievements. You are not a victim of too little time, as though it were some sinister creature. Rather, you are master of your time. Often, the best and most productive word to affirm your control in this area is "no."

Even as you want to assist everyone who requests attention from you, it may be best to say "No." You really help yourself while serving others in the name of Christ by being wise in your time management. The following example might illustrate this point.

Whenever our church has a major event (renewal worship, afternoon outing, and the like), I counsel married women of our congregation to complete their regular household responsibilities before the event: dusting, doing laundry, changing linens, cooking, vacuuming, and more. That way, a saved (or unsaved) husband will not resent the church and pastor for taking their wives away from home for extended periods of time. In the New Testament, Titus 2:1-5, Paul offers exhortations of domesticity.

2) Time Must Be Allocated to Important Works

As I alluded to above, there are some prolific megachurch pastors/authors in America. Faced with thousands of congregants, multiple staff members, decisions, Bible studies, sermons, hospital visits, counseling sessions, and other stressful demands on them, they must be persons of rigorous scheduling. I would venture that each has particular days/times for significant functions: family devotions, prayer, exercise, meditation, reflection, hospital visits, counseling, sermon preparation, envisioning the future, leading marriage ceremonies, officiating memorials, and more. No doubt, a key component must be the process of compartmentalizing. That is, every significant activity must fit into one's overall life function.

Clearly, some leaders have staff to handle certain matters, freeing them up to achieve what only he/she can do. Time-management thinkers refer to such as delegation, with the expectation of integrity, professionalism, dignity, and full accountability. However, as former President Harry S. Truman reminded all, "The buck stops with the leader."

At the same time, Christian ministries of all sizes should not neglect the vast hordes of volunteers in any congregation. They add an immeasurable supply of willingness, experiences, gifts, talents, insights, and more.

Volunteers (many of them retired workers) bring years of secular insight, creativity, organization, punctuality, and professionalism to the multiple tasks/ministries of a progressive, successful twenty-first-century congregation.

3) Operate in God's Guidance; Trust Him to Give You Sufficient time

Hopefully, my next statement will not be construed as rude or mean-spirited: I am glad that some people do not have time for all their pursuits. Because if they had the time, they might tear down the world! Negative, toxic, dehumanizing works should not fit in your daily, weekly, monthly, or yearly schedule!

On the other hand, monumental tasks could be blessed by some sense of "extra" time. As an example, Christian theologians debate the events of Joshua 10:12 and following in the Old Testament. I am inspired by this Joshua 10 narrative, as Joshua literally commands the sun and moon to cooperate with him. Audaciously, he seeks "more" time to succeed in his venture for the glory of God. Liberal scholars will suggest to us that he was speaking metaphorically, arguing that cataclysmic events would have occurred if this were literally true. At the same time, conservative scholars would note that when you invoke the name and power of God, He works in mysterious ways. Whatever the case, the Bible offers the definitive footnote, "There was no day like that before it or after it, when the LORD listened to the voice of a man; for the LORD fought for Israel" (Joshua 10:14).

Perhaps in mundane pursuits, you might accomplish more if you'd simply and profoundly invite the Master of life to guard, govern, and guide your time each day!

4) Ask Achievers How They Succeed in a Frenetic, Fixed Time Frame

In various parts of this book, I reference "go big" people from various disciplines, both secular and sacred. The questions often posed to them are, "How do you do it all?" "How do you pray, work, recreate, dream, and achieve?" "When do you have the time to study the Word, love your family, invent, coach, write, compose, act, or sing while finding time for hobbies, family, and your friends?"

Without straining the matter too much, supra-achievers quite often "find" time by excising the trivial. You will never reach higher mountains while mired in the trivia of life. Now, people and their hurts are never trivial! Each of us exists to make deposits in the lives of others. Yet, a great deal of what you give your time to, in critical analysis, is quite trivial.

5) Ask Trusted Family and Friends to Hold You Accountable for Your Time

Due to conflicting demands on your time, it may be beneficial to share your plans with a small cluster of wise, intelligent, godly family members and longtime friends. Your intent involves inviting them to be your sounding board for moves and actions before you make monumental plans. For example, if you want to enroll in classes at the local community college to position yourself for a job promotion, then tell that accountability group. In the days leading up to enrollment, one from the group might ask you, "When does school begin?"

Never view any question from them as invasive, pushy, or rude. A response of "none of your business" would ruin the connection. Instead, view their questions as the compassionate concern of those who love you. They also evidence those who want you to succeed in the venture that you initiated!

6) Master Your Time, or It Will Master You

Think long regarding a matter. When does it have to be completed? Now, make your commitment to attain it. Get it done immediately, for waiting may prolong or prevent its attainment.

Within this context, allow time for divine interventions. That's when God stalls you or puts someone in need in your way. Don't be selfish; nothing we do is more important than meeting the needs of others. Achievement for ego gratification alone is, in my view, secondary to the hurts and sufferings of others. Though it might sound trite, life is more about donation than about compensation. And, as followers of Jesus Christ, we serve others!

I am sure that psychiatrists, psychologists, and therapists would assert that stress often comes from feeling overwhelmed by the multiplicity of challenges attendant to twenty-first-century life. That life regularly brings about anxiety, pressure, and uncertainty.

Let me add to the problem: your stress may be the result of God's pushing you beyond what you can fulfill in your own power. Time then seems tyrannical; you must meet time-consuming demands from family, friends, and others. Because of that feeling, God wants you to lean on His inexhaustible resources (worship, prayer, meditation, reflection, fasting, Bible study, giving, service, and sharing faith in Christ).

7) Procrastination, in the Name of Patience, Is Really an Excuse

In candor, one of my major problems involves procrastination, putting off important and not-so-important matters until a later time. Unfortunately, you will not enter the arena of "go big" with such an attitude. Rather, you must savor and seize every moment. As a spiritual coach, in the name of Christ I push others (and myself) to fight the tyranny of procrastination. Whatever you need to do, go do it right now!

I live in recognition of the brevity of human existence. Just a moment ago, I peered over three pictorial directories of our church membership. In sixteen short years at our church, I have seen small children become youth, youth become married couples, young couples mature, grandchildren added to the family dynamic, and all of us become grayer with thinning hair—or in my own case, go bald altogether! Without our permission, time moves at a rapid pace.

So daily, we engage the enemy called "tomorrow." I asked a friend for a favor. I fully expected that he would execute my request in a timely manner. Instead, he counseled that I should be patient; it would be possible to achieve the matter, literally, tomorrow. I was not very happy with that response. (Interestingly and ironically, in an earlier case he asked me to compose a professional letter of recommendation for him. I did it immediately!)

Therefore, even as a maturing Christian filled with faith and confidence in the timing of God, I was pained that my friend would in such a cavalier manner dismiss my request for urgency in my matter. Procrastination works that way. It convinces you that time is your ally rather than your antagonist. Great achievers never allow themselves the luxury of the easy "later" or "tomorrow." To the world's credit, they are people of "today" and "right now."

Sometimes, I wish I didn't know the accepted, conventional wisdom of "let it breathe" or "wait a while," because in some cases, the best strategy might be to "take the leap." Implicit in that injunction is *right now!*

However poorly, I am simply trying to convey the idea of taking decisive action even without all the relevant data, trusting God to furnish more details as Christians "walk by faith, not by sight" (2 Corinthians 5:7).

Indeed, some will never fail in life precisely because they never tried. Against that proposition, place me among those who might experience awful failures, but at least I will also be among those who may achieve at heightened levels because I was unafraid to try!

8) Proper Use of Your Time Glorifies God

Since none can determine the length of life—ten, thirty, fifty, or eighty years—it is wise to use every day allocated to us by the Almighty God to honor Him. At the end of each day, you should ask yourself, "What did I do today that honors the One who gave me the great gift of another day on earth?"

The psalmist captures the essence of my concern: "So teach us to number our days, so that we may present to Thee a heart of wisdom" (Psalm 90:12). Within that verse, I do not see pathos, sorrow, or morbidity in the face of eventual death; instead, I see vibrant possibilities in living life!

If life really is a bestowal from God, then for a Christ follower, every minute, every hour, every day should be utilized for advancing the kingdom of God through Jesus Christ. Even as a secularist, the short span of any life should cause you to commit your time, energy, and resources to something high and noble, something that constitutes a cause greater than yourself.

To "go big" in almost any endeavor, I encourage you to carve out time in your busy day—after work, perhaps—for creative reflection. Past watching a drama, the news, or sports on television, you might read a newspaper or a few chapters of a serious book. In the process, you will expand your vocabulary, discover deeper insights, and authenticate sources of information. The pithy saying holds true, "Readers are leaders."

I dare not close this chapter on time management without offering a word from a persuasive thinker, Victor Hugo. The French poet, novelist, and dramatist of the Romantic Movement opined, "Short as life is, we make it still shorter by the careless waste of time."

Or you might benefit from Hugo's further exhortation: "He, who every morning plans the transactions of the day, and follows that plan, carries a thread that will guide him through a labyrinth of the most busy life."

Though Hugo's worldly wisdom in words does not reach the level of Scripture (see the opening of this chapter), perhaps they will convey substantive truths for all to consider.

Therefore, you might ask yourself a few practical questions:

- Where did my time go?
- Who/what stole it?
- Did I neglect something essential in favor of something convenient, easy, or fun?
  - Now lost, how can I get my time back?
  - How must I make better use of time tomorrow?
  - What, really, is the best usage of my precious time?
  - Will my words about time match my willingness and works?

Please permit me a closing thought on time. As of this writing, I am at the mid-point of my life (mid-50s). Daily, I note friends and family being called home to rest in the arms of God.

During my twenties and thirties I was less inclined to reflection, because in my immaturity there was so much to accomplish and so much time in which to get it done. Savings. Material things. Grand achievements. By my forties, by God's grace, I could see the outlines of a spiritual legacy, the proper utilization of the time God had allocated to me.

A few years ago, a brain tumor scare awakened in my spirit the brevity of life, and this thing we call "time." It became clear that every day could be my last one!

At this juncture, I can't waste a day. Facetiously, I tell our church, my family, and friends: "I don't buy green bananas. I need ripe ones to eat, today!"

Earlier I referred to my life stage as "mid-point." That means I plan, by God's grace, to finish this race called life—spiritual, scriptural, strong, steadfast, substantive, while striving for more—with excellence!

Again, I encourage you to "go big" by using wisely the precious gift from God called time!

CHAPTER 9

Go Big: Environment and Exposure

If you are anything like me, you have noticed the recent proliferation of talk shows, life coaches, self-help books, tape series, lectures, and conferences. Purportedly, they share an agenda of teaching, motivation, inspiration, and leading you to the proverbial "next level" of attainment. As many in America are still mired in mediocrity, something is definitely wrong. These efforts prove futile because, absent personal responsibility resulting in intentional engagement, you may read the literature, attend the conference, buy the teachings, and remain stuck in neutral.

While "go big" resonates in your spirit as a clarion call to grand achievement, it rings hollow until you critically examine what makes such achievement possible. Some, in my view, will remain mired in the state of "gonna," without reaching their articulated goals. Part of that reason for sustained inertia may stem from being and staying in the wrong *environment*, without *exposure* to better thinkers. Let's consider these interrelated concepts.

1) Assess Your Environment

"Environment" references the aggregate of surrounding things, conditions, or influences. It embodies what impacts you from the outside over against what guides you internally. It involves an important setting for substantive engagement if you operate from the "go big" proposition.

Theoretically, esteemed colleges and universities serve as rigorous academic environments with undergraduate, graduate, and doctoral students occupying the rarefied air of lecture halls, exploring theory, research, exams, reflection, and collaborative discussions under the influence of Nobel laureates, renowned scholars, esteemed guests, and adjunct professors. Not surprisingly, golden institutions (Harvard, Yale, Princeton, Brown, MIT, Stanford, and Columbia, for example) annually produce leaders in the arts, politics, jurisprudence, medicine, journalism, business, and world affairs.

In these academic environments, admissions officers choose from those who have completed STEM courses, who also have off-the-chart SAT scores and interesting backgrounds, having defied odds while juggling numerous extracurricular activities. By any measure, such students are uniquely prepared for professional success.

In America, corporate leaders in banking and law emerge from a select group of schools. Historically, the majority of U.S. Supreme Court justices graduated from Stanford, Harvard, or Yale law schools. Wall Street is dominated by a coterie of graduates from the business schools of the same universities, who pledged the same fraternities and will serve together on corporate boards as they eventually marry educated women from their unique social circle. Environment, then, helps define the contours of high professional success.

Environment, further, is significant for substantive achievement because it becomes contagious, as success breeds success. Often, you rise because others around you rise as you desire more from life, aiming to maximize your potential. Quickly, based on environment, you take advantage of opportunities while learning to seize the moment.

2) Evaluate Your Environment

In the large picture of life, you need to thoroughly evaluate and, when necessary, change your environment. Literally, you may work a full year while anticipating your ten-day Caribbean cruise in early summer. In the process, you save money, envisioning the white sand and azure waters. Still at home you are, in many respects, changing your environment. If you put on some reggae music, the transformation is almost complete. After the actual trip, the expectation is your return home—thoroughly refreshed and reinvigorated—with pictures. In the aftermath of the adventure, you are revived, reanimated, and renewed, ready for all that comes forth.

For others, you may not fully change your environment, but at the least you should desire a cleansing of the environment in which you usually operate. Perhaps "air" around you has become polluted and foul. Negativity, cynicism, gossip, and jealousy may be its manifestations. Perhaps "water" around you is contaminated by impurity, filth, and debris. Again, none of this proves helpful for your mental well-being. Perhaps "soil" around you is infested with toxins or known carcinogens, preventing healthy vegetation from growing there. If any of these are true, your environment will adversely impact your outlook and judgment.

My advice to you is this: become a radical "environmentalist," particularly concerned with conducting regular assessment of the pollutants, people, and perspective of the environment in which you live. Once you do so, real and lasting change is possible for you.

3) Manifestations of the Wrong Environment

In truth, you may sincerely yearn for a better, more productive life, yet you remain ensnared in sameness; you languish in small ambitions because of your surrounding conditions. When you make substantive changes, sociologists call it escaping a tough, adverse, challenging environment. For example, if you aspire to graduate from college, becoming the first in your family to do so, it will be difficult, yet not impossible. Family members may wish you well in academia, but without a full sense of its rigors, their advice may be useless beyond a point. Yet, if you give optimal effort (applying, getting admitted, and disciplining yourself in engaged studies while staying connected to other student-achievers), that's the first step in changing your environment.

For others, your change might be committing to marriage while the environment around you affirms "hook-ups," serial relationships, casual dating, and cohabitation. Again, if you want traction, purpose, and success leading to wealth building, marriage remains the best antidote to poverty while aiding ascent up the ladder of success.

I am quite aware of people who express all the right words for change, for increase, for better conditions, and yet seem hopelessly trapped by and in bad choices, unhealthy habits, weird situations, and negative outcomes. I sincerely pray that you are not among such persons. Please do not live with an excuse for every negative thing that happens to you.

Why does excuse making come so easy to many? One reason this continues to happen (and perhaps it happens to you) is the tendency toward intense contact and foolish conversation with those given to low ambitions. If you remain around negative people, that negativity will enter your spirit, fouling your mental environment. Subtly, your speech patterns will become littered with their phrases, capitulating to ignorance, defeatism, fatalism, profanity, and other manifestations of the wrong environment.

4) Escaping the Wrong Environment

Of course, the answer to your wrong environment sounds simple: just change your surroundings. The difficulty, however, involves an existential break from long-term friends, family members, coworkers, or people with whom you have become comfortable. Maybe the best idea is to take a few days off from people! Discover your own joys, peace, and fulfillment in solitude. I know: you may be uncomfortable, even afraid, of spending time alone, charting out your path.

Honestly, if you are intimidated by an empty home, see it as your refuge, your place of introspection. Once you look inward, you discover strengths you never knew about yourself. Once you look inward, you learn what you can achieve by the power of God and your own determination. Once you look inward, you face down the demons of depression, debt, and doubt. In your solitude, you become a better person.

Another recommendation for escaping the wrong environment is to literally write out your personal mission statement describing who you are and the objectives you seek to implement in a life of success. In this mission statement, attach times and dates for achievement as useful targets for action. It is advisable to commit this mission statement to a responsible friend (an achiever!), as he/she will hold you accountable for making those benchmarks. Give that person permission to challenge you at regular intervals if you fail to live up to your dedicated mission in life.

5) Embracing a New, Right, Positive Environment

Your new environment must be stimulated by insightful reading, which cultivates fresh ideas. Television, radio, Internet, and social media represent passive attempts at acquiring information; you listen while absorbing depictions of timely ideas, trends, and events.

On the other hand, reading good material involves active mental acuity (thinking!). Again, reading requires time, energy, effort, and engagement with important ideas, trends, and events. After thorough reading, you will be forced to ask yourself questions: "What does all this mean for me?" "Where is all this going?" "How should I change my behavior?" "How much of this relates to my destiny?" "Can this material fuel my passions?"

6) Cultivate a Changed Environment

Admittedly, I cannot fathom how intelligent people can refrain from quality time spent in reading the Bible, novels, biographies, memoirs, histories, newspapers, magazines, and more. I am well-aware of those who work long hours in a stressful environment and commute home in heavy traffic. After all that, you may want to change apparel, eat dinner, and relax after a taxing day. In place of reflexively turning on news or soothing music, I offer an alternative: allocate the same time as you would give to news or music to a great read.

Reading changes your environment, as it stimulates your mental energy and fosters your latent creativity while transporting you to new worlds. In the process, your knowledge increases, your mind races, your vocabulary expands, and you enjoy vicarious experiences while discovering life beyond your own narrow experiences. Moreover, if you commit to regular reading, in short order you will gain confidence in expressing your views, joining with other national and global "thought leaders" who are well-read and articulate.

7) The Christ-centered Environment

For still others, your new environment refutes selfish living, coming to faith in Jesus Christ. This decision must be immediate and definitive, aided by an earnest plea to God. Only when you confess sin before Him, renounce it, and ask for new life in Christ will your life change for the better! Sundays go better when you discover the joy of worshipping God, celebrating His grace and power among other Christians. Consider me old-school; worship in a church sanctuary with other believers facing daily struggles supplants being "at home with my Bible." Connected with the concept of corporate worship, when obstacles arise you can rely upon determined, maturing prayer warriors who call upon the name of Jesus.

I pray you are not among those seeking a new environment without noting the supreme importance of the spiritual dimension (embracing Christ) as the summit of your concerns. Nothing intellectual, relational, professional, material, or personal will ever change for the better unless and until you recalibrate your relationship with God through His Son, Jesus Christ.

My life assignment from God involves prompting you toward a fertile, healthy mind as an intellectual being. I am a committed advocate for your college/university admittance, anticipating your professional attainment. Encouraging good, healthy, affirming, positive, dynamic relationships also is part of my responsibility from God.

At the same time, if you honor God, work hard, and work creatively while making kingdom investments in people and worthy institutions, I celebrate your material prosperity. Highest of all, I pray you walk in spiritual alignment with God, which only comes through acceptance of Christ as Savior and Lord. When you know, love, and obey the incredible God, it transforms the entirety of your environment, both from within and from without.

"Go big" people, then, are very careful regarding the environment around them. You must, at all costs, avoid environments that are not conducive for fresh ideas, new approaches, or enhancement of your creative capacities. If life is to change for the better, I advise you to have an honest, tough conversation, not with others, but with yourself.

8) Environment Connects High Aspiration and Hard Work

At the same time, a good environment explains the connections between high aspiration and hard, sustained effort. When you are part of a striving, thriving community of achievers, it becomes normative that you, too, will bring your intellectual and interpersonal gifts to bear. Your aim for excellence will be sharpened by your environment. In this regard, I am reminded of two brothers born from the same parentage. One remained in his chaotic, gritty, tough, urban setting. On the other hand, his brother went to live with relatives in the bucolic suburbs. The results from the different environments in which each came of age are startling. Today, one is a professional; the other is, twenty years later, still "trying to find himself."

A wholesome, positive, affirming environment can change the trajectory of your ambition as you await an assist from the culture in which you operate. When people around you applaud success while exhibiting "fruit" themselves, it electrifies the atmosphere as you learn to function among other achievers. Indeed, you feel strange if you lack a story of success, a long-range objective, or some basis for feeling accepted in this grouping.

Here is an illustration that crystallizes this point. Early in Christian ministry nearly forty years ago, I joined with three other young men who were earnestly pursuing God as eager, neophyte Christian ministers. One Sunday evening after worship, we decided to enjoy a snack together, planning to eat while dreaming together regarding our collective futures in the ministry. This late snack turned into several hours together. It was an environment ripe for reciprocal blessings. Each of us left that pivotal conversation energized for the ministerial journey that lay ahead. None could predict where the providence of God would take each of us.

Today, with much gray in our hair (if we still have hair!), we are yet serving God, representing Christ, walking in grace, and giving our all to God's people as mature Christian leaders. We serve in various faith communities across America as senior pastor-teachers. All of us, humbly, are seminary graduates, and a couple are published authors. Praise the Lord for His works!

From an environment of young dreamers, throughout nearly forty years of Christian ministry the four of us have faced various challenges without wavering in our commitment to spiritual enrichment of God's saints or lessening of dedication to advancing the kingdom of God through Jesus Christ. Truly, our spiritual relationship affirms the Word, "Iron sharpens iron, So one man sharpens another" (Proverbs 27:17).

When one has been unusually blessed, the other three share in that joy. Conversely, when one has been in need (personal pain, death of family members, ministry challenges, and so forth), the other three are there, providing whatever is necessary. Our friendship and its duration are rare in ministry, particularly, and in life, generally.

Equally valid, you must see the connection between environment and exposure as vital prompts toward your "go big" ethos. You must appreciate the interplay of these concepts. Let's consider it:

9) Understand the Value of Exposure

"Exposure," in its literal sense, means to lay open to danger, harm, as to the air or cold, as in subjecting photosensitive material to light. Think of old-fashioned (before cellular phones) camera film. It also involves widening parameters, or transcending limitations.

For our purposes, "exposure" references necessary contact with and learning from important sources of information and insight, stimulating extraordinary observations of reality beyond the norm. It also challenges conventional wisdom, fueling new discoveries. In grappling with the notion of exposure, we need an illustration of it. Let us consider the following one.

The governor of the state of Florida hosted a luncheon for a group of clergy where we discussed the plight of children and youth in the foster care system in his state and nationally. Along with twenty others, I was blessed to share in the festive luncheon. The luncheon was catered, with each place setting done in elaborate detail. This entailed each participant's being seated before his/her name card, beautiful plates and saucers embossed with the Florida state seal, several forks, knives, spoons, crystal stemware, and linen napkins. Oh, and the food was very tasty! Such a display of class made me want a well-set table at every meal!

A substantive PowerPoint presentation expounded upon the realities of foster children in need of loving adoptive families. We committed ourselves to alleviating that problem by encouraging more families to take orphaned children into their homes and their hearts.

Exposure fostered our discussions with the governor of Florida. We were pastors with passion, working for the needs of children languishing in the foster care system. After meeting with that governor, we were ready to visit the Oval Office in Washington, D.C., as the plight of millions of needy children continues to be a national challenge.

10) Actual Travel Enhances Exposure

Here is another concrete example of exposure. A man traveled to London, England. While there, he visited iconic historical sites: Big Ben clock tower, Westminster Abbey, Tower Bridge, Buckingham Palace, Parliament, 10 Downing Street, and more. During his leisure, he dined on codfish and chips. Wanting to please his wife, he shopped at world-famous Harrods for just the right gift. With curiosity piqued, he strolled through beautiful gardens, a landscaper's dream for meticulous precision. Afterward, he walked past graveyard markers of famous and infamous historical figures.

Prior to his London excursion, this man had not traveled a hundred miles from the place of his birth. After his foreign trip, he was a better specimen of himself: more confident of global travel, more familiar with airport and customs regulations, and more welcoming of others with differing ways, accents, and habits. In fact, he told all, "As a result of my trip, my life will never be the same again." What changed everything for him? It was exposure to another country, culture, and its citizens.

If you want more from life, it starts with leaving home. Yes, that is a tough assertion, but you can immeasurably grow once you leave the nest. Away from those you know and love, you will discover internal capacities you never really knew. Consider that you could travel to nearly two hundred countries around the world. Understanding the economics involved, I nevertheless encourage you to widen the parameters of your knowledge through some travel. If you fear the airplane, how will you lead a life of achievement? Remember, high achievers are invited to speak, teach, and lecture about their respective areas of expertise.

In the Old Testament, God revealed an awesome plan for a nation He would birth through Abraham. There was only one stipulation from God: Abraham had to leave home! (see Genesis 12:1). In the process of moving from the familiar, Abraham became a mighty man of insight with progeny who would change the world! But it all started with wider exposure, literally leaving home.

11) Exposure Demands Breaking from the Familiar

Exposure takes you from the familiar to the unfamiliar while furnishing you with new tools (conceptual, visual, and visceral) for navigating a different set of circumstances. If you enjoy a dream vacation in an unknown country, upon your return you, too, will be ready to visit another desired locale, be it domestic or foreign. The extent of your dreams often is proportional to the scope of your exposure.

"Exposure" takes you into new psychological territory, with the ability to weed out false from authentic phenomena. Your reasoning and analytical abilities are honed by greater association with certified successes in varied ventures. That might represent a definition of your mentors in life. Indeed, the value of mentors in promoting your achievement must be repeatedly emphasized. Interfacing with noble minds leads to a clearer vision of possibilities, elevating the human spirit as well as the human condition. Allow me to share a few insights into one who served to mentor me, establishing a paradigm for "go big" in my heart.

I am blessed by God because I came under the influence of a person who relentlessly pushed me, exposed me to all of the possibilities of God working in my life. However, if I hadn't internalized that exposure as the prelude to greater things to come, I would simply be a fortunate individual and not an achiever.

12) The Right People Foster Greater Exposure

During my early teenage years, my life was radically altered when I came under the spiritual and godly influence of the wise, compassionate, and renowned Christian leader Dr. Edward V. Hill of Los Angeles. He was a pastor, preacher, leader, and strong champion for the cause of Christ. Literally, thirty weeks of any year, he would preach during Sunday worship then leave town on Monday to fulfill a prominent speaking engagement in another part of the country or in another part of the world.

Upon his return, he would regale our congregation with all God had done (Christian organization before whom he preached, seminary where he lectured, keys to a city he received, political figures consulted, colleagues on a national conference panel, and more). We were enthralled, congratulatory, and moved that God would so widely use our pastor for His glory while advancing the kingdom of God through Jesus Christ.

For me, these reports served as an introduction to the limitless dimensions of Christian ministry. I learned that God could so choose to use a human instrument in spreading the Gospel of Christ to unsaved humanity. Later, the exposure God gave to my pastor was foundational in what I expected God to do for and in me after I surrendered to the divine call to Christian ministry in 1978.

Indeed, I initially thought every preacher received a thousand invitations per year to proclaim the Word, across America and globally! Of course, I later learned this was not the case. Now I understand that I and that congregation were highly favored by God to come under the shadow of such a seminal Christian leader.

13) Unusual Experiences Heighten Your Exposure

Exposure actually puts you in the room with luminaries as they discuss topics of concern, with global implications. At the invitation of my pastor, I was in a hotel suite with him, Jesse Jackson, and other national figures as they discussed the possibility of Jackson running for U.S. president in 1984. It was not then and is not now important that Jackson didn't win the presidential nomination. It did, however, stun the nation with its audacity (intentional word used by a succeeding candidate in 2008). I mention this episode because these kinds of events reveal how minds are enlarged through exposure, illustrating unknown possibilities.

If you are a younger person, I would advise when exposure opportunities present themselves, you should take mental notes of the persons involved. Recognize the import of the discussion, the way luminaries comport themselves, the gravitas involved, and more. If you find yourself in such dignified company with significant participants, this is definitely not the time to state your opinion. Rather, express gratitude to God and whoever invited you for the privilege of up-close observation of their proceedings.

14) You Must Fight Inhibiting Factors to Exposure

Exposure celebrates hometown heritage and small-town values, but it refuses to revel in narrow vistas, knowing that greater opportunities often await you when you leave home, literally and metaphorically. The aphorism captured it well: "Once a mind has been expanded by greater exposure, it can never return to its original dimensions." When you try to lead others without having adequate exposure, you limit the group, as one limited person relates to others. Yet, it is also true that to some degree a little exposure exceeds none at all: "In the land of the blind, the one-eyed man becomes king."

You must resist and repudiate parochial notions. There is no basis for boasting if you conquer a circumscribed domain. If you operate within a fixed area with a single racial group, social class, or known subset of people, you will not enjoy the infinite possibilities of exposure. Celebrate a national or global perspective. When you fear encroachment from the larger, unfamiliar, hostile world, you will tend to retreat to that which is easy, comfortable, and familiar. In a literal sense, then, you need a change of scenery.

I trust that you are not among those who lack curiosity regarding other countries, new ideas, different people, hairstyles, customs, cultures, attitudes, and more. Indeed, America represents an amazing country, the envy of the world, the only military/economic/freedoms super-power. Yet, America is just one of two hundred nations, globally. When you travel outside her borders, you understand the value of greater exposure to the world beyond you.

Moreover, asking "What if?" may rankle some, as they know all the possibilities, but you will never learn if you fail to engage in discussions with others, exploring all angles of a situation. If something, or someone, tries to inhibit your curiosity, and, therefore, your exposure, vehemently fight against these.

Your "go big" moment may be when you awaken to the strictures holding you down, chief among these being a lack of exposure.

15) Exposure Immeasurably Contributes to Your Success

You may note that an increasing number of U.S. veterans are being hired by companies. Both because of patriotism and the unique skill sets they seek, companies place higher value on veterans. Most veterans, further, exhibit qualities associated with exposure: professionalism, punctuality, perseverance, discipline, loyalty, ability to follow instructions, teamwork, neatness of appearance, character, integrity, and more.

You should also view exposure as the capstone of a complete life. If you have "been somewhere," or around those of greater exposure, you will express appreciation for all that you have. I learned gratitude to God for all He had given me by visiting several poor countries around the world. What Americans throw away, in many cases, would be gladly retrieved by others the world over.

16) If You Really Want Achievement, Savor Exposure

"Exposure" produces an insatiable desire for accomplishment as you have witnessed it in others with similar backgrounds, flaws, insecurities, and doubts. Once you recognize the fact that, in most cases, the true geniuses have already been identified, you can then join the rest of humanity, starting a business, writing a book, finishing college, owning a home, breaking free of debt, having a real relationship, giving your all to Christ, or worshipping God regularly while seeing bright horizons for the future.

Now, you must set yourself to the harder task of making those objectives a tangible reality. What separates people—leaving some as idle dreamers, while others draw closer to fulfillment—involves the degree to which you commit to and work toward your stated goals.

Years later, I still savor my one experience flying on a chartered private jet. A friend invited me on a trip with a few others. All of us had enjoyed commercial first-class, but this private jet was completely different! We didn't have to pass through elaborate security screening (no wand, no stares, no pat-down, and no removal of shoes). Instead, the limousine (yes, he provided that too!) took us directly to the waiting jet. Once in-flight, unaccustomed to this level of luxury, I decided to remain quiet, watching all the other passengers. Whatever they did, I followed. It was a great flight, and I thoroughly enjoyed every minute of it. Now, I am unable to feel the same travel experience when I fly commercial. Once you've been exposed to more, it will do that to you!

17) "Go Big" Occurs, Indisputably, through Your Exposure

Over the last decades, you have probably heard the "go big" philosophy uttered at a conference, from a lecturer, or from a book. Though excited about it, afterward nothing substantive emerges from your declaration of intentions. This breakdown concerns me, as I hope it does you. If you are really concerned about the "high" of the conference, lecture, or the book, followed by the "low" of the afterward reality, then you will take decisive action.

The renaissance you are seeking begins with the decision, which means you obtain the information as to the start of the new semester at the community college; and, as two friends (more than sixty years old) did, enroll in classes. Or it means you will go to the gym, pay the price and join, and then anticipate good results (stress relief, a trimmer physique, getting rid of that belly, and so forth). Or it means writing the business plan, going to the bank, and filling out the loan application while scouting different areas for vacant buildings for your new business. Indeed, there must be some urgency, or else you will languish in the planning mode. I sincerely trust you will not be a victim of the "paralysis of analysis."

"Go big" sounds great for youth, young adults, and those early in their careers. Presently, I am in my middle years, yet I am excited about the "go big" ethos. Whatever your age or stage of life, you can adopt it as well. Sixty-five-year-olds are running marathons! Seventy-year-olds are finding their true love! Eighty-year-olds are exploring social media, posting to Facebook, watching YouTube, and tweeting!

18) Once Exposure Takes Effect in You, Embrace It

Likewise, the reason you can embrace "go big" is your recognition that God's grace has enabled you to live in your present. Therefore, He wants you to integrate your environment and exposure in order to fulfill a lifelong dream.

Even with the proper combination of environment and exposure, you must maintain a driving purpose in life, one higher than simply obtaining credentials for inordinate material wealth in the form of second homes, artwork, yachts, private jets, stocks, mutual funds, and exotic vacations. If those are your only benchmarks of success, then you will awaken one day to anxiety, depression, and frustration, searching for deeper cosmic significance. You should never sacrifice health, relationships, exploration, fun, and curiosity while searching for deeper meaning. Truly, deeper meaning is found ultimately in your relationship with God as you leave something tangible reflective of your ideals and the institutions you treasure.

I conclude this "go big" chapter with an antiquated notion: *noblesse oblige*. It means that the good life is defined as the development of moral character, intellect, sensitivity, and devotion to a cause for the benefit of others—one sure to outlive you. Indeed, you need a holistic curriculum of the accumulated wisdom of great ideas, books, theories, and controversies which have shaped the culture in which you now live. Your focus should entail acquiring the tools, not only for a good livelihood but, more importantly, for a good life.

When I attend or officiate at memorial moments (funerals), I quickly scan the obituary or life portrait printed of the deceased. I am seeking the extent to which the person was exposed and what they did with that exposure. Some day in the future, the same will occur for you and me. Important life questions will include these: "Did he/she learn from other cultures; visit other countries; acquire broader skills; interface with other ethnicities; contribute to ideals/ideologies/institutions; stand for moral principles; or wage worthy battles?"

In short, wide exposure will compel you to achieve the "go big" ethos you are familiar with. Little or no exposure will result in little or no achievement. Some people just want more because they have seen more. I trust you are in that category!

For example, two men discussed a younger colleague who had a good education, moral code, ambitions, and more. The elderly men conversed as to the best means of helping the young man toward success. One said to the other, "It's obvious that he will, one day, make his mark in life. Like a seamstress, we must sew him up, according to the pattern of his exposure."

That's my objective in the chapters of this book: remind readers of their inherent potential and worth in God, their "go big" opportunity. Then, I pray to "sew" you up toward unimaginable achievement for the glory of God, the advancement of His kingdom, and the celebration of Jesus Christ culminating in enhancement of the human condition.

CHAPTER 10

Go Big: Enthusiasm and Epiphanies

In pursuit of permanence for the "go big" ideal, we should add to our recipe the critical ingredient of enthusiasm. Nothing beneficial or lasting comes to you without enthusiasm for it. The "it" in life proves illusive if you pursue with lackluster interest. For example, if you pursue a romance, you must exhibit enthusiasm toward the object of your affections. Wooing another requires incredible amounts of time, energy, and, critically, some finances (for dinner, movie, shoes, purses, cologne, and so forth). If you need employment, the human resources officer discerns your level of enthusiasm. At the very least, your online application signals interest. Yet, that must be followed by frequent calls of inquiry. Then at some point, there is an in-person interview.

If you really want a particular home in just the right neighborhood near the high-ranking school system, you must express enthusiasm, or else another buyer will quickly close on it while you dither. If you yearn for emotional and psychic healing from God, enthusiasm shows itself in the magnitude of your prayer, Bible study, and yearning.

This talk of enthusiasm should not be confused with some rash, impulsive streak, but rather, a due deliberation followed by readiness to act. "Go big" requires another explanation of enthusiasm: willingness to go all in. For you to achieve on a large scale, you must pursue such vigorously and resolutely. On the other hand, if your effort is half-hearted, it will not sustain you nor draw allies to your cause. Life will reward you, and wonderfully so, if you will make the extra effort, going beyond what is expected.

As I write this chapter, I am just returning from a day-long workshop led by a distinguished scholar of eighty-five years by the name of Dr. Cecil "Chip" Murray of Los Angeles. This dynamic octogenarian serves as adjunct professor at the University of Southern California. USC is a nationally ranked university with a tremendous endowment, respected professors, and enviable research facilities. Over the years, I have avidly followed Murray's career. His constant has been an enthusiasm for principles and a lively defense of beliefs. Despite changes in his field and changes in the culture, he has maintained vigor while adapting to this new world order. While in Kansas City recently, I listened as he taught. His insight was keen, illustrations timely, grasp of current trends sharp, his mind quite fertile.

Some his age might well delight in working their gardens, relaxing in an easy chair, or just raging against the ravages of time. Others might commence a victory tour, reminiscing regarding past victories. Uncharacteristically, this leader exhibits enthusiasm for his discipline. Like Caleb in the Bible in Joshua 14, this octogenarian remains a compelling voice and force, still relevant for the present generation. (If you are older than eighty, don't allow anyone to call you old; just tell them, "I am an octogenarian." When they return with its definition, you will be long gone, occupied by unusual acts!)

I am inspired by leaders like him as they still dress as professionals, still remain abreast of current events, and still believe that the power of an original idea combined with strategy and work are the necessary components for the "go big" life.

In Joshua 14, Caleb teaches generations to follow him in critical lessons in faith toward God. There, he expresses

1. a *faith* that never *wavers*.
2. a *strength* that never *weakens*.
3. a *conviction* that never *wanders*.
4. a *love* that never *wanes*.
5. a *purpose* that never *withers*.

For a birthday present, Caleb asks Joshua not for a party, nor for candles, nor for a cake, nor for a song; rather, he asks for "hill country." At eighty-five, he retains mental acuity, depth of perception, stamina, fortitude, daring, courage, dedication, memory, spiritual sensitivity, integrity, character, focus, drive, and determination.

Interestingly, the hill country of Hebron represents the area the spies some forty-five years earlier had argued was the most dangerous, containing the giants before whom ten of the spies cowered as a "grasshoppers."

So on his birthday, Caleb asks Joshua to allot him the rugged terrain that was the toughest area in Canaan. By this request, he signals his aim to subdue a formidable area. Imagine an amalgam of rocks, stubble, hard ground, cracks, crevices, and dry creaks; and Caleb specifically asks for that area.

Though I am considerably younger than my esteemed instructor or Caleb, each inspires me to "finish strong" with enthusiasm intact. I have (and you, too) no legitimate excuse for diminution in intensity, or vigor, or focus on the things that really matter.

The "go big" mentality is driven by relentless enthusiasm. Let's consider the greats of entertainment and athletics as one example.

1) Relentless Enthusiasm Illustrated

The late, great Frank Sinatra, master showman, will be long remembered as the saloon singer, brooding over loves come and gone. As Old Blue Eyes grew older, with adoring fans of all ages, wearing an elegant tuxedo, a shot glass of whiskey on the stage, he was later christened the "Chairman of the Board." To the end of his career and life, he enjoyed filling venues as a consummate entertainer. Las Vegas hotel stages were his home turf, even as he concluded national performances with the iconic song "New York." Into his eighties, Sinatra maintained his swing and swagger, snapping his fingers to the pulsating, big-band rhythms.

Equally true, Sammy Davis Jr. lifted audiences with voice, dancing, coolness, gusto, enthusiasm, and charisma. Ahead of his time, he integrated Las Vegas dark rooms on the basis of his supreme talent. He illustrated to the world that "Mr. Bojangles" could ease, if only temporarily, their cares. Again, to the end of his career he entertained. He exemplified the truism "If you enjoy what you're doing, it isn't really work."

Long after he had retired from an illustrious career in baseball, Joe DiMaggio demanded that any public introduction of him include the words "The greatest living New York Yankee player." Following these words, he would amble out of the dugout to thunderous applause. This introduction prevailed to the end of his life! That is the definition of enthusiasm for the game.

While researching contemporary evidence of enthusiasm in the world, the *New York Times* (8/23/14) profiled a man named David Spector. The story describes him as an American-born comedian and talk-show host in Japan. Owing this distraction to a grueling schedule of numerous appearances on shows there, Spector's public persona exudes what the article refers to as "boyish enthusiasm," despite his undisclosed age (probably late fifties). Further, he is cited for sheer durability, using one-liner jokes delivered in flawless Japanese. Note his assessment of his own popularity: "I've earned my stripes just by outliving everybody." Clearly staying the course and staying true to core principles exudes enthusiasm.

In like manner, you must integrate availability, accessibility, visibility, and reliability for the attainment of profitability. When you are fully engaged, ready to serve before the people, and standing in integrity, glorious things will ensue. Though you are not a child, the concept of "excitement" should still resonate in your spirit. No matter your age or stage of life, you have important tasks to complete. You never become "old" unless or until you surrender your mind, heart, and will.

2) Wisdom Interacts with Your Enthusiasm

Since wisdom comes from God as well as from analysis, observation, experience, and engagement, when you reach the point of having something truly profound to express, limitations of the mind and body may render you hesitant to state it. This is nonsense. Instead, well-received teachers should be those still possessed with enthusiasm, still fresh in their approaches, still connecting with all generations.

Enthusiasm, I submit, fuels the "go big" paradigm because so often you can miss the shift. Sadly, you could watch the parade of history rather than being an active participant in it. Or you could tell the present generation of its responsibility to seize the moment even as many remain clueless as to articulating a vision for humanity. Even when you are uncertain of the full extent of the destination, at least you should give a signal as to that direction.

In sports, the coach is charged with charting the course for a team. When he says "Here is what we should do," it does not mean that every play will be successful. In the game, however, someone must announce the play. Someone must take authority while being accountable for the outcome. Else, excellent athletes will be left to their own discretion. This is the plight of present-day America.

Too many (I trust not you!) are too careful, never aiming high for fear of failure. That very timidity threatens our national and global life. Instead, allow your enthusiasm to soar to heights unknown. Of course, the realities of life will bring some ideas down to earth. Yet, for a brief, fading moment, wouldn't it be nice to contemplate how far the "go big" ethos might take you?

3) Enthusiasm Clashes with Cynicism

Inevitably, enthusiasm clashes with cynicism. "That won't work" represents the easiest way to thwart innovative concepts. Despite the fact that it has been debunked as a successful strategy, you might intermittently fall prey to its devastating impact. In fact, I hope you join me in pity for those so small in their thinking that the only way they can feel alive is by killing others' dreams.

Repudiating doubters, real enthusiasm embodies serial "reinvention," as you make yourself indispensable to your friends, colleagues, neighbors, community, city, state, or nation. The response of those who may not be inclined to consider your merits or to work with you is astounding: "Wow, is she still around?" "I thought we saw the last of him five years ago?"

Even after sickness, challenge, or major life upheaval, reprise the immortal line, "Reports of my demise are greatly exaggerated!" Indeed, enthusiasm explains your staying power; through it all, you have weathered storms, faced doubts, and overcome fears while trusting in the invisible hand of God. For that, you are now wiser, stronger, resilient, and better.

When the "go big" ethos becomes permanently embedded in your psyche, it fuels your enthusiasm, for often you must rely upon little more than your internal resources. People around you, if not similarly on your "go big" path, may serve as seemingly implacable obstacles to your progress. Early on, you must learn the value of dogged determination if you aim to achieve. Truly, it is incredibly important that you understand the scale of your life arc, the stupendous proportions of what you are undertaking.

4) Your Waning Enthusiasm Empowers and Emboldens Doubters

In many ways, you can empower and embolden your doubters by the expression and example of internal vacillation. People yearn for well-informed, strong, decisive leaders. Too much analysis by you, without direct engagement, will heighten mistrust in your power to attain your objective. Thus, I advise you to openly celebrate small victories on the way to the ultimate achievement.

Your celebration of small victories inevitability warns all around that you intend to remain with the task until its fruition. Often, that warning may be necessary for you! Progress comes because you will not give in to your doubts, your uncertainties, your lack, or your struggles.

At the same time, I offered two pieces of advice to a political candidate: 1) Your enthusiasm stimulates my faith in your candidacy; and, 2) If there is anything negative waiting to come out regarding you, you should frame the issue first before anyone else does.

5) Your Enthusiasm Must Be Self-generated, Self-contained, and Self-evaluated

When the "go big" motif is alive in you, it needs daily enthusiasm, starting with your convincing yourself that despite what you may face, the objective remains worth it!

I serve God and His kingdom as a family man, Christian pastor, preacher, teacher, lecturer, and as a writer. As a family man, I encourage my wife in her professional pursuits; my son in his college studies; and my daughter in her brilliant world. Friday night is Family Night, with my daughter choosing the restaurant. (Even at her young age, she chooses the most expensive ones!)

As a pastor, by the aid of the Holy Spirit I must produce compelling messages and targeted Bible studies (in print) for a growing congregation. Also, I must pray, counsel, visit the sick, comfort the bereaved, share the vision of progress, encourage giving toward our budget, manage the staff, supervise our outreach efforts (programs and people), prepare for weekly radio/online outreach, while attending ministry gatherings, and more.

As all Christian pastors should, I believe God has uniquely positioned our ministry in Kansas City for dynamic service to advance His kingdom cause. I give our ministry my full attention. I accept blame for any shortcomings. In humility before God, I share in our successes for the glory of God. I subscribe to a simple philosophy: leaders must lead! Daily, I am optimistic and enthusiastic. Our congregation knows it well: every Lord's Day, we aim for new souls for the kingdom of God. Being people-centered, my enthusiasm bubbles over!

As a teacher, I derive supreme joy from breaking down biblical concepts. In the process, I hope to illustrate points of application for daily living. In our local congregation, I have developed written studies for all our classes. We aim to build Christian disciples through intentional intake of the Word of God, practical illustrations, and obedience to godly principles.

Donning the hat of a Christian writer, for a potential audience of thousands or millions, I assume an entirely different responsibility: develop a sound, biblically true, theologically based, Christ-affirming, positive, anointed, dynamic, coherent theme.

Every book I have written (ten and counting) has been a veritable war with myself. The blank computer screen dares me to complete a coherent thought. "Now," it beckons, "what about a sentence?" Then, it demands a paragraph. After I feel satisfied with a paragraph, the screen still dares me to complete a chapter. Now, it dares ask, "Can you finish this book?" As I share with friends, it is never easy!

Enthusiasm for each book project, then, must be self-generated. If I fail to spend three to four hours each day devoted specifically to it, I will not finish on time (the clock for completion is also in my head!). A colleague, aware of the demands of a growing ministry, asked when I found time to write books. In truth, I do not know. Full disclosure: reading is my hobby, so as I read, new insights aid my research. Book ideas mysteriously present themselves, daring me to plunge in.

6) Your Enthusiasm Will Determine Your Schedule

When you are enthusiastic about some pursuit, you find time for its enjoyment. Indeed, if you relish that pursuit, nothing will prevent you from engaging in it. Time, indeed, represents a precious, limited commodity. Yet, my golfing friends find time in their busy schedules to make a tee time of 6:00 a.m.! The same holds true for those who enjoy basketball, tennis, or racquetball. No matter the weather, they find pickup games. This is equally true for dominos, chess, or backgammon aficionados, who most always keep a set or a board handy, "just in case."

Those who travel the world also find time for its enjoyment. The tedium of airports, security lines, baggage delays, customs, or currency exchange rates will not deter them. At the same time, you discover that time marches onward. Some pastoral colleagues enjoy hours of drinking coffee with Christian colleagues, wondering why people don't attend worship as they did in bygone days. While that time spent might refresh and recharge the spirit, I have an alternative suggestion for tangible church growth. Pastor, what you need instead is a biblical, practical, personal evangelistic plan to increase visitors and foster new members.

The simple truth you need is to learn to prioritize while discovering what you and only you must do. The rest you should leave to others. That's delegation. In all that you do, still, if you are a leader, then you are accountable to God, to the people you serve, and to yourself for an excellent job.

Increasingly in the twenty-first century, you can feel overwhelmed by demands from your job, family obligations, household chores, day-to-day bills, and millions of other stressors. Without enthusiasm for some worthy pursuit (hobbies, gym visits, nature walks, club meetings, yoga, relaxation, and so forth), you dance on the periphery of fatigue, lethargy, and futility. From corporate America, we hear references to achieving the proper work-life balance. I recommend you find what really heightens your enthusiasm and fervently chase after it! Then, you will celebrate not only a balanced life but also, more importantly, a productive one.

Incredibly, those overwhelmed, if they find something which piques their enthusiasm, will find energy to engage with it.

7) Your Enthusiasm Will Often Surprise Even You!

As you envision a new reality and a few parts of it come into view in tangible form, it fundamentally alters your future. You will start believing in it fully. What may have started as an abstract reality will transform into something that has limitless potential. Victor Hugo said it well: "Nothing proves invincible against an idea whose time has come."

Once you have been knocked down and you discover the power from within to get back up, you are truly embracing enthusiasm. The anonymous quote holds true: "Life is short; live it. Love is rare; grasp it. Anger is bad; dump it. Fear is awful; face it. Memories are sweet; cherish them. Victories are possible; seize them."

Another quote begs permission to refuel your enthusiasm. Since the quote ignited my heart, I shall offer it to you: "Nobody ever wrote down a plan to be broke, fat, lazy, or stupid. Those things are what happen when you fail to plan."

Enthusiasm pushes, prods, and prompts you to expend time, energy, and effort in any worthy objective designed to refuel what life robs from you. Whenever you feel depleted, it results from an inability to recharge your enthusiasm. Never rest until you discover your passion, for in that passion resides an unquenchable enthusiasm. Professional athletes playing children's games are, in fact, pursuing passion. The greatest ones do so with unbridled enthusiasm. Watching them run, jump, chase, contort, yell, and scream, you see enthusiasm oozing from their pores.

If you face challenges (and we all do!), you will eventually search for adequate coping mechanisms. As stated earlier, you will allot time and energy in the earlier engagements, along with art, music, classes, and other diversions.

No matter where you discover diversions, they must be moral, legal, and ethical; and you must embrace them with gusto!

Indeed, the stressors you face will never relent in their intensity. The challenges of life, then, grow tougher each day. So you elude their pernicious impact to your mental and physical well-being by enthusiasm for something fun, different, and stimulating. You break the monotony by stepping outside your routine. If not, you fall into a rut. Someone defined a rut as a grave with the front and end omitted. Ouch!

After a surgical procedure followed by a sufficient period of recovery, I resumed a full workload. A friend challenged me with these words: "Now, I want you to take off one day; go to the movies. Put on some jeans. Pick a silly, funny movie. Don't analyze it, just watch it. Just change your routine." I followed his advice. It was therapeutic. Afterward, I felt refreshed. It was, as the ad says, "my beach."

Similarly, you should find your personal beach, where you can express your enthusiasm.

8) If You Observe Keenly, You Will See Epiphanies

Unexpected pleasures represent life's epiphanies. They represent, in my view, memoranda sent from heaven, exposing hidden joys in small moments. For example, a rainbow, a sunset, a warm breeze, a beautiful butterfly, a galloping deer, a babbling brook, an out-of-the-blue call from a friend, a letter from afar, a warm reunion—they are all epiphanies. Add to that list the spectacular sunrise in the east, registering the dawning of a new day. When you feel down in despair, remember: God is ultimately "up to something."

Woven into the normal are reminders of the divine presence. When enthusiasm ebbs, you need an epiphany to raise your spirits. At just the right moment, God intervenes with a manifestation of His wonder. The psalmist said, "O LORD, our Lord, How majestic is Your name in all the earth" (Psalm 8:1).

My longtime brother in Christ and global preaching treasure Dr. W. Franklyn Richardson of New York calls such times "oh" moments, finding them scattered throughout Scripture. By another rendering, God drops down to His children in particular, and humanity in general, what I call "epiphanies."

I encourage you to slow down, as epiphanies occur every day. Some call them accidents, coincidence, luck, right place, or "a funny thing happened to me" moments. Without debate, I affirm them as epiphanies from heaven, where a divine lesson becomes intertwined with normal events.

9) Life's "Wow!" Factor – Epiphanies

By nature, I am optimistic. Through salvation in Christ, by my walk with God, by His enabling power, I choose to view the glass as half-full rather than half-empty.

Some call it perspective; I call it absolute faith in God. With $5 in your pocket presently, choose to reflect on the faith you have; by next week, through God's grace you will have $50. You need that same faith in order to interpret an epiphany.

When you interpret it, it produces a "Wow!" factor. God intervenes in your thoughts, showing your heretofore unseen phenomena reflective of His grace toward you. Those are epiphanies. Take time in your busy schedule to observe one of those gifts from heaven. Your appropriate response should be "Wow, Father, You did it again!"

10) Cultivating Epiphanies

Reading books, engaging in conversations, observing what some call "nature," visiting new cities, trying new experiences—all of these serve as soil for epiphanies. You should savor these moments. Think here of the mighty redwood trees, standing as sentinels in Yosemite National Park in Northern California. These are gathered epiphanies, reminding us of the grandeur of our God. Again, Wow!

Wisdom teacher Dr. Mike Murdock popularized the saying first, I believe, followed by others: "If you want what you already have, keep doing what you have always done. Conversely, if you want what you don't have, do what you haven't done." Within those words, seek God's epiphanies for your journey.

If you properly assess and interpret these miracle moments, God will reveal something sublime that nurtures your enthusiasm, reminding you of the rightness of your course, confounding detractors, steeling you against intimidation, easing travel toward your destiny. In fact, destiny should not be confused with destination, for you are experiencing destiny right now, while you live.

When you fully grasp this "go big" concept, you appreciate the connection of enthusiasm (about your possibilities in life, in general) with epiphanies from God. The former represents an innate sense of the purpose of life, while the latter involves God's affirmation of it. Endowed with the mammoth nature of our God, the "go big" instinct becomes normative thought.

Though often misunderstood, I have found that "go big" people, fueled by enthusiasm and focused by epiphanies, will inevitably move toward that intangible magnet: faith in a coming achievement.

To his contemporaries, Dr. Martin Luther King Jr. was a peerless orator, organizer, and leader. His famous August 1963 dream for America in general and blacks in particular was not realized in his lifetime. Yet, we now understand the genesis of that dream: enthusiasm and epiphanies coming together.

If the thousands (black and white) attending Dr. King's funeral in 1968 had been willing to dream with him, his struggle to lift America from the quagmire of segregation, racism, hatred, violence, and despair would not have been so difficult!

Today, then, facing your own challenges, since you have read thus far, I know you are well on your way to the "go big" transformation. Yet, you must read on for more principles!

CHAPTER 11

Go Big: Creativity and Charisma

Within the matrix of all that leads to the realization of the "go big" ethos, we must not undervalue creativity. Creativity takes you from original concept to tangible culmination. Because you and I were created by the Creator in His image and likeness, we express creativity. Indeed, you are creative whether you recognize it or not.

As I reflect upon this dynamic, I am reminded of professionals who have recognized their creativity: architects, interior designers, poets, musicians, artists, and others. In each case, these persons envision an unseen reality, then they bring it to life for their own pleasure and for the benefit of others.

As with other latent traits, creativity must be honed and sharpened through practice, frustration, failure, discipline, adherence to well-established professional standards, learning the rudiments, and serving an apprenticeship. After many years of travail, you may be accorded credentials, respect from peers, compensation, and deference as a leader in your chosen field.

When creativity lags, what should you do? For the definitive answer, we must always direct attention to the repository of revelation, the Scriptures—the inspired, inerrant, infallible, authoritative Word centered in Christ. There, we discover the way through the thicket of challenge, using creativity at every marker. What, then, can creativity do for you?

1) Your Creativity Grapples with Problems and Perplexities

When you are sincere in your "go big" sentiment, you need a strategy for success; you must prepare for problems and perplexities. No matter your objective, if it were relatively easy someone would have achieved it long before you attempted it. Creativity, however, maneuvers around problems. You do well, in my view, to anticipate every possible challenge. As an optimist, you should expect the best while, paradoxically, preparing for the worst. Let's consider a few examples of what I term "creative pragmatism."

In air travel today, creative pragmatism suggests it is wise to get to the airport early to circumvent a host of issues: full parking lots; boorish parking monitors; lack of curbside baggage attendants; rude security personnel; abrasive flight agents; late arriving planes; delays in service; cancelled flights; cramped seats; inconsiderate passengers; nonexistent or terrible food; misplaced keys, cell phone, personal computer, or tablet; no bin space for carry-on luggage; and more. So you save yourself considerable angst by previewing these possible inconveniences well before your next trip.

Faced with the above travel possibilities, I purposefully schedule my arrival time for a speaking engagement or conference early enough so as not to have an immediate conflict if the airplane on which I am traveling proves to arrive late at my destination. If this occurs, the hosting group becomes nervous, wondering if my late arrival will jettison a well-crafted conference or event. So the remedy is to prepare for a possible delay. Also, a speaker should cushion in enough time for a brief respite at the hotel or a holding room before standing before an audience. Of course, if your arrival was delayed as the fault of the airline, a caring speaker would at the very least apologize for and briefly explain his/her tardiness. It's called manners and common courtesy.

Another scenario that requires creative pragmatism involves personal finances. You receive your weekly, bi-weekly, or monthly compensation. Before the month is over, unfortunately, you may discover shortages, preventing you from meeting your obligations. One remedy: live according to a written, detailed budget. Then, pay all obligations immediately, in alignment with receiving weekly, bi-weekly, or monthly compensation. So if bills are met early on, later in the month you may be low on cash flow. This should not pose a problem, as you have already met your obligations.

For those who ridicule the notion of living paycheck to paycheck, I reply thusly: In America's stagnant economy, it is a blessing from God to still receive a paycheck!

Even if your compensation, perhaps as a couple, exceeds $10,000 monthly, you still need a good budget. A budget should include revenue, expenses, and future plans. Even after you complete a budget to guide your financial affairs, add a category for emergencies. For some, these emergencies (plumbing repairs, appliance breakdown, auto repair, high utilities, child's needs, insurance deductibles, and more) are dealt with through their savings or a credit card. The general idea involves having financial structure in your life, personal discipline, and anticipating occurrences you cannot foresee. I advise that you live life with a sense of "just in case."

A third challenge engendering creative pragmatism involves personal or psychological threats. Here, the concern involves meeting any situation with poise, grace, courage, and fortitude. Your temporary struggles must never be met by permanent solutions. I am reminded of those who contemplate or actually commit suicide because of depression, debt, disease, divorce, or other distress. All of those are temporary challenges; the solutions come in the change of a new day, another week, another month, another year.

Gospel artist VaShawn Mitchell offers wise counsel in his song "Turning Around for Me." He sings of the change God can and does bring about for those in right relationship with Him through Jesus Christ. Note this persuasive part: "I can see the breaking of day, God is making a way. A change is coming for me, if I stand strong and believe. There's no reason to doubt; I know He's working it out, and it's turning around for me. And it won't always be like this; the Lord will perfect what concerns me. Sooner or later, it'll turn in my favor."

While there are any number of challenges that might come against you, the general point holds true: exercise creative pragmatism, whatever it is. I am emphasizing a nimble quality—being ready to adapt, to alter the plan despite what may come against you. The Boy Scouts creed holds true: "Always be prepared."

2) Take Lessons from the Ants

While musing on the general idea of creativity and especially what you should do when creativity lags, I was led to a biblical teaching which references an analogy from the ant world. In the Old Testament, we note these soaring words:

> Go to the ant, O sluggard, Observe her ways and be wise, Which, have no chief, Officer or ruler, Prepares her food in the summer *And* gathers her provision in the harvest. How long will you lie down, O sluggard? When will you

arise from your sleep? "A little sleep, a little slumber, A little folding of the hands to rest"—Your poverty will come in like a vagabond And your need like an armed man. (Proverbs 6:6-11)

On its surface, this proverb may not seem deep or profound, nor poised to yield grand insight. After all, it centers on an ant! However, if you deeply probe Proverbs 6, its principles will astound. Consider a few of them.

First, ants (small, wingless insects) work well beyond their physical capability. You witness this as ants somehow carry particles of food upon their backs. In fact, the food may weigh more than the ant! Instinctually and creatively, the ant maneuvers the food, hoisting it, carrying it, and depositing it.

Second, ants are not regimented in their actions by rank, chain of command, elaborate organizational apparatus, nor the knowledge of eventual outcome. Instead, relying upon dexterity and cunning, nimbleness and versatility, ants operate.

Third, ants demonstrate tremendous resilience, seen in their ability to reengage after their molehill is stepped on by frustrated humans. Patiently, however, ants rebuild as they are continually drawn to a sweet, sticky spot on the kitchen floor. Nothing (short of mopping or using bug spray) seems to deter, dissuade, disturb, or defeat them.

Fourth, ants, rather than resting and cruising in the summer months, work! Proverbs 6:8 affirms that the summer represents a busy time for ants. They prepare their food in this season, instinctively anticipating the lack that winter will bring.

Fifth, ants operate from an antipoverty stance, in that their work ethic (non-idleness, infrequent sleeping) demands constant action. They prepare prior to need!

So in substance, ants teach us the value of creativity, personal responsibility, resilience, and a healthy work ethic. Famously, Frank Sinatra sang of the determination of ants in his song "High Hopes." With so many filling street corners in America, I am convinced you still need a confluence of those traits for successful outcomes.

3) Your Creativity Shines Brightly amid Adversity and Anxiety

Somehow, you have been duped into having the idea of enjoying a positive, happy, stress-free life. As you mature, chronologically and spiritually, you quickly discover that life represents a never-ending series of adverse and anxiety-producing experiences. Once this assertion is accepted, you must marshal the mental, emotional, and volitional tools to meet them.

Let's quickly acknowledge it: adversity happens! Christian families face pain, hurt, and suffering. Good people must cope with extreme challenge. Nice people experience reverses, lack, and impoverishment. Children, even godly ones, can drive you to your knees. Men shirk leadership roles, hurting wives and imperiling families in the process. Women dishonor and disrespect their mates. Parents grow old. Death is life's common denominator. The demands of this world never cease. Indeed, if not for God and our relationship with Him through Christ, we would drift along like a ship without a sail!

In any of the cases presented above, anxiety becomes a daily reality. In our hectic, frenetic, callous, and coarse culture, everyday events induce anxiety. In your psyche, you sense that foreboding, intimidating, on-the-edge-of-your-seat, wondering-what-will-come-next instance. Most times, you are bombarded by a barrage of negativity (murders, rape, corruption, inhumanity, genocide, terrorism, protests, and more). In such times, again I remind you to develop new skills and coping mechanisms for the new challenges you face.

One important skill to master is the ability to stay in the moment. This means you are attuned to what presently faces you. Don't look back or ahead with anxiety. Don't preview what has not presented itself. When challenges come, meet them. Particularly, Matthew 6:25-34 contains principles applicable for you in living a meaningful life.

Another skill for combating anxiety involves learning to reinvent yourself along your journey. You should never be so wedded to a situation, a tradition, or a perspective that you cannot reformat when presented with new information. You remain up-to-date, focused, and dynamic by adapting to new situations. When your circumstances change, you must change. The only idea and ideal that never require reformation involve God's honor, His grace, salvation in Christ, and the Spirit's regenerating power, all for the advancement of the kingdom of God in individual hearts.

4) Your Creativity Expresses Nimbleness of Mind and Spirit

It is absolutely critical that you develop a nimble mind and spirit so as to cope with ever-changing realities. The only constant in life is change. In football, for example, a running back must constantly watch for changes in the defense, moving quickly as would-be tacklers approach. Standing still will result in the running back suffering a loss of yards. In much the same way, I encourage you toward watchfulness, ever-ready to assess new variables in your life situation.

I approach technology in this way: when a new cellular phone, tablet, or portable computer comes out, I exchange the old for the new. I sense that new capabilities and new apps will be available with the latest technology. It is refreshing to know that "go big" leaders and personnel in Silicon Valley are constantly envisioning and bringing to the market new ways to enhance life for consumers.

5) Your Creativity Is Instinctual and Impulsive

Often, you will not recognize your creativity until you have tried and failed in some noble venture. Consider that an old inventor reached a conclusion on the one-hundredth attempt: "Now, I know ninety-nine ways this will not work!" His invention became the product of his instinct and impulse to forge ahead, despite multiple failures.

At the same time, you need to trust your instincts. Major crimes have been solved because a detective had an instinct or a hunch without vast evidence upon which to base it. Something just didn't "sit right" with the detective. Late at night, her or his instinct began to piece together the outlines of the crime: placement of body, time of murder, cause of death, forensic evidence, suspect, motive, opportunity, history with victim, past threats, or lack of alibi. So he kept searching for connections in available bits of information. Then, perhaps, he brought in a suspect. After questioning, he took his "hunch" to superiors and an arrest was made. By the time of trial, this instinct was augmented by, say, a confession and a preponderance of other evidence.

6) Your Creativity Must Rise against Its Ultimate Challenge

I cite another Old Testament narrative here as an example of creativity in action. Please note the verse: "If you have run with footmen and they have tired you out, Then how can you compete with horses?" (Jeremiah 12:5a). The prophet, resolute in faith, is yet troubled by an age-old perplexity: Why do the godless prosper? Inability to solve this vexing enigma placed insurmountable hindrances in Jeremiah's way. If he cannot resolve this matter, it may imperil his service for and to God. In response, God warned of greater consternation, befuddlement, and opposition from others. Meaningful life for you pivots on discerning your identity: "footman" or "horse."

In today's language, God's reply to Jeremiah raises the issue of creativity. Indeed, when you cannot fully resolve a conundrum, it should prompt enhanced thinking toward a solution. As attorneys declare in court regarding indisputable facts, "We will stipulate to . . ."—so bad, immoral, and vile people will prosper in this life. And you may not always obtain returns commensurate with your investment—relational, financial, emotional, or otherwise. You should stipulate to those realities.

At the same time, you must harness creativity to the degree of your righteous indignation relative to a situation that may not change. Since the situation may not change in the foreseeable future, the question becomes relevant, "What must you do, knowing the facts at hand?"

Don't just get angry regarding a negative situation. For example, indignant mothers made a difference as too many people were binge drinking and then driving, injuring or killing others. MADD (Mothers Against Drunk Drivers) is the national organization resulting from that indignation. Over the years, they have become ardent advocates for safety on American highways and roadways.

In other words, "go big" striving recognizes life's unfair scenarios (good things happen to "bad" people, and bad things happen to "good" people). Despite such truths, your creativity must reach toward the level of Jeremiah's "horses," knowing that you were not fashioned to merely run with "footmen." Note the stark contrast.

Horses, notably thoroughbreds, prance with a distinctive gait, propelled by the sheer force of their instinct, weight, size, and strength.

Observe their hind legs, moving like pistons, oblivious to any threat. Internal pride prevents intimidation from external challenge. People wager large sums on such horses, living vicariously through their exploits on the track. In horseracing, small jockeys ride stout stallions to victory. If I may be so bold—to succeed in life, you need "horse" sensibility and sensitivity.

Footmen—soldiers, boots on the ground, the infantry—on the other hand, can only make progress when well rested, well fed, and well motivated. Take away any one factor, and they fall prey to a greater enemy. Soldiers, further, are human, defined by vexation, vagaries, and vicissitudes of life. Thus, victory in a military engagement is contingent on their whims, flaws, idiosyncrasies, and deficiencies.

7) Your Creativity Awaits New Ideas and Paradigms

I enjoy the blessing of a rich, long-term friendship with a like-minded, beloved, sharp, anointed pastor in my area. Frequently, we meet for lunch and stimulating discussion. We operate from the premise that 1) we love God; 2) we aim to advance God's kingdom in Christ; 3) we love the work we have been called and ordained for; and, 4) we are immeasurably assisted in Christian ministry through associations, books, articles, ideas, and conferences built on paradigms of spiritual achievement.

Out of those times together, the fountain of faith is replenished. I recommend the same for you, as you are just one step away from a great idea. Your days are enhanced to the degree that you surround yourself with innovative thinkers and acclaimed achievers. Part of your challenge involves moving from a spectator watching others succeed, to being a participant allowing God to monumentally achieve using the vehicle of your life. As many soar to great and grand heights, good creativity asks, "Why not me?"

8) Discover Your Creativity in Observation of Others

As a Christian, I begin every evaluation of the inspired, inerrant, infallible, authoritative Word of God with a prayerful desire to discover and then to implement biblical principles culminating in Jesus Christ, for any undertaking. For example, when I analyze the "go big" philosophy, I am reminded of the Master's disciple Simon Peter. The Gospel narratives reveal Peter as a case study of flaws, faults, and failures, yet he also exemplifies faith dedicated to Christ despite setbacks.

"Go big" creativity provoked Peter to walk on water while his comrades enjoyed the safety of their boat (see Matthew 14:28-30). It also led him to articulate the foundation of the Lord's church (see Matthew 16:16-17) without rabbinical or theological training. He was just a fisherman! It later inspired him to suggest building three tabernacles on the mountain even without any tools (see Matthew 17:4)!

Still later, Peter vowed to remain in Christ's fold only to deny Him three times (see Luke 22:33, 56-60). Perhaps ultimately, the grace of God crowned his daring demeanor and passionate pursuit by allowing Peter to preach the Gospel of Christ on the Day of Pentecost (see Acts 2), as three thousand souls were added to a fledgling fellowship of Christ followers in one day!

As I evaluate God's employment of Peter as a disseminator of truth centered in Christ, I am elated as He deposits His treasure in "earthen vessels" (See 2 Corinthians 4:7). The truth is abundantly clear: God gains glory through broken, deficient, flawed creatures giving their all to advance His kingdom in Christ. And as I hope you are in a similar spiritual status—forgiven, born-again, redeemed, and justified—there is hope for you! Indeed, if Christ could employ Peter as a recipient of divine grace resulting in new life in Christ, there is hope for you!

Creativity, then, yields to another critical component for attaining "go big." I am thinking now of a display of charisma. Let us carefully evaluate this character trait as an operative principle for success at the highest levels. Developing a working definition of *charisma* will aid our efforts.

9) Charisma Defined

Charisma represents a special quality of leadership that captures the popular imagination while inspiring unswerving allegiance and devotion. In popular culture, it is associated with presence, swagger, or sizzle. It is more readily recognizable in extroverts, while it may be more challenging for introverts to display it. In more rarefied settings, we emphasize savoir faire, confidence, heft, poise, grace, authenticity, self-assurance, and spontaneity. When pressure builds in a stressful situation and you express decisiveness, you exhibit a critical aspect of charisma. It serves to defuse an intense moment, often with wit, charm, or well-placed, self-deprecating humor.

In an article in the *Wall Street Journal* (8/6/14), *charisma* is described thusly:

> There is one in every office—the person who gets the attention of senior managers and interns alike at the morning meetings, who sends out witty tweets in the afternoon and who glides effortlessly through the after-work cocktail party, never at a loss for words. What is this person's secret? It boils down to presence, a magical mix of confidence, charm, and communication skills that exerts an outsize impact on one's social status and ability to climb the ranks.

Charisma, then, reflects special qualities—intangibles—giving you outsized influence over large numbers of people. Often, it represents an "it" factor. Further, it involves a combination of energy, dynamism, surprise, originality, imagination, shrewdness, deftness, tact, perspicacity, articulation, and more. Finally, it may remain undefined: you simply know it when you see it!

Further, charisma embodies personality traits including optimism, drive, forward-looking ability, freshness, liveliness, and creativity, projecting that personality onto others like a contagious disease. Ultimately, as leaders you persuade others toward a course of action.

10) Charisma on Display

Fifty-plus years after John F. Kennedy's assassination in Dallas, Texas, in November 1963, historians and pundits still search for the best words to describe charisma, a hallmark of his short but successful presidency. Was it riches, youthfulness, a large family, Harvard training, influential advisors, witticisms, self-deprecating humor, made-for-television good looks, a beautiful wife, picture-perfect children, a sunny disposition, or some combination thereof? Or was it the vaunted legend of Camelot, with projections of "what could have been"? Or was it

America's obsession with star quality? In many other avenues, charisma demonstrates itself. Consider other examples from various disciplines.

11) Wide Range of Leaders Endowed with Charisma

Charisma reflects itself in corporate America, as Fortune 500 companies take the advice of head-hunting firms that make CEO and other key position recommendations based on vision, intellect, experience, and professional reputation. While it may not be explicit in the job description of a successful candidate for CEO, charisma proves essential to swaying a large company or entity. Indeed, by the extension of charisma, CEO and company become inextricable. Think Jack Welch of GE, Bill Gates of Microsoft, Larry Ellison of Oracle, Steve Jobs of Apple, Jack Ma of Alibaba, or Mark Zuckerberg of Facebook.

Equally true, in professional sports the best leaders are conversant in the Xs and Os of coaching, yet charisma plays a prominent role in producing a team of championship-caliber players. In professional basketball, we note Arnold "Red" Auerbach, Phil Jackson, Pat Riley, Glen "Doc" Rivers, Michael Jordan, Earvin "Magic" Johnson, Julius "Dr. J" Erving, and a few others who possessed that charisma gene.

In golf, we relish the charisma-driven exploits of Ben Hogan, Sam Snead, Arnold Palmer, Jack Nicklaus, Tiger Woods, and Phil Mickelson among others.

In baseball, true aficionados celebrate Babe Ruth, Ted Williams, Joe DiMaggio, Jackie Robinson, Satchel Paige, Dizzy Dean, Willie Mays, Mickey Mantle, Sandy Koufax, Hank Aaron, Reggie Jackson, and Derek Jeter among others with that illusive "it" factor. Charisma, superior performance, and heart separate athletes from legends.

In football, many revere Paul Brown, George Halas, Vince Lombardi, Chuck Knoll, Bill Belichick, Fran Tarkenton, Johnny Unitas, Joe Namath, Jim Brown, "Mean" Joe Greene, O. J. Simpson, Gayle Sayers, Walter Payton, Deion Sanders, and others with on-the-field and off-the-field charisma.

In Christian ministry over the first half of the twentieth century, those endowed with charisma include William Seymour, Karl Barth, Billy Sunday, Dwight Moody, Reinhold Neibuhr, and others.

Later, spanning the last sixty years, we must add the Christian preaching legends Billy Graham, William Sloane Coffin, Edward V. Hill, C. A. W. Clark, Martin Luther King Jr., Charles Stanley, Chuck Swindoll, Jerry Falwell, Adam Clayton Powell, Bill Bright, D. James Kennedy, Chuck Colson, Gardner Taylor, Paul Morton, Tony Evans, Rick Warren, T. D. Jakes, Joel Osteen, and many others. Combining divine calling, integrity, biblical exegesis, scholarship, theological insight, folksiness, unique preaching gifts, vision, organizational skills, prophetic genius, personality, and more, these individuals reached national and global acclaim.

Further, in entertainment, several unique actors and actresses captivate screen and stage, primarily due to their charisma. Stage legends included Helen Hayes, Lillian Hellman, Tennessee Williams, Lorraine Hansberry, Langston Hughes, Noel Coward, James Earl Jones, Cicely Tyson, and others.

In the golden age of Hollywood, we note luminaries such as Jack Warner, Cecil B. DeMille, Alfred Hitchcock, Billy Wilder, Orson Welles, Humphrey Bogart, Lauren Bacall, Barbara Stanwyck, Tony Curtis, Jack Lemmon, Elizabeth Taylor, Richard Burton, Marilyn Monroe, Sidney Poitier, Lena Horne, Clark Gable, Marlon Brando, and others.

Closer to the present day, we celebrate Samuel L. Jackson, Jamie Foxx, Denzel Washington, Meryl Streep, Julia Roberts, Will Smith, Halle Berry, Sandra Bullock, George Clooney, Robert DeNiro, Al Pacino, and others.

Over the last half-century, charisma boosted the journalistic careers of such notables as Edward R. Murrow, Walter Cronkite, Theodore White, David Broder, Dan Rather, Peter Jennings, Barbara Walters, Diane Sawyer, and many others. Daily before millions they informed the nation through interviewing newsmakers and reading the news while personifying integrity in reporting it.

In the comedy segment of entertainment we see the power of charisma in the influential careers of Stan Laurel and Oliver Hardy, William "Bud" Abbott & Lou Costello, Redd Foxx, Phyllis Diller, Bill Cosby, Lenny Bruce, Richard Pryor, George Carlin, Joan Rivers,

Johnny Carson, Jerry Lewis, Bob Hope, Jack Benny, Red Skelton, and others.

Of more recent vintage, we note the career trajectory fueled by charisma: Jerry Seinfeld, Robin Williams, Eddie Murphy, Steve Martin, Martin Lawrence, Chris Rock, Steve Harvey, and others.

In popular music, the annals of twentieth century history are replete with those in whom charisma dwelt: Thomas Dorsey, Duke Ellington, Frank Sinatra, Ella Fitzgerald, Sarah Vaughan, Dean Martin, Sammy Davis Jr., Miles Davis, Quincy Jones, Charlie Parker, Ray Charles, Elvis Presley, and others.

Closer to the present, we note the musical genius of the Beatles, Stevie Wonder, the Rolling Stones, B. B. King, Eric Clapton, Kenny Rogers, Dolly Parton, Diana Ross, Aretha Franklin, James Brown, Michael Jackson, Barbara Streisand, U2, Luther Vandross, Whitney Houston, and many others. What linked them all together was the indefinable, irrepressible "it" factor.

In jurisprudence, there have been icons known for courtroom finesse, legal insight, theatrics, and, of critical importance, charisma. In the early twentieth century, the list includes Clarence Darrow, Felix Frankfurter, Earl Warren, Thurgood Marshall, and others.

Closer to current times, we note legal eagles such as Earl Higginbotham, Constance Mobley Baker, F. Lee Bailey, Alan Dershowitz, Johnnie Cochran, John Roberts, and a slew of others.

Among military leaders at the highest levels, revered for courage, determination, patriotism, skill, military genius, and valor, we must not minimize charisma as recent history celebrates George Patton, Dwight Eisenhower, Douglas McArthur, William Westmoreland, Colin Powell, Norman Schwarzkopf, and David Petraeus.

In American literature—both poetry and prose—America celebrates phenomenal persons of letters acclaimed because of talent, influence, and charisma: Ralph Waldo Emerson, Nathaniel Hawthorne, Emily Dickinson, Henry David Thoreau, Edgar Allan Poe, and others.

Closer to contemporary times, the erudite literate revere Ernest Hemingway, Gore Vidal, Norman Mailer, James Baldwin, John Updike, Toni Morrison, Nikki Giovanni, Maya Angelou, and others.

Returning to politics, certain U.S. presidents over the last fifty years were unusually blessed with charisma: John Kennedy, Ronald Reagan, Bill Clinton, and Barack Obama. While others were elected president during the same time frame, these few leaders—despite diverging perspectives, shifts in society, scandals, agendas, and administrative challenges—were able to impact the country in unique ways.

Ironically, these named presidents were able to be elected and re-elected by sizable margins. Of course, Kennedy was assassinated while in his first term. (Notably, I would argue George W. Bush and Richard Nixon lacked charisma, even as they were twice raised to president. We would call them anomalies.)

Perhaps one of the keys to electoral success in American politics involves being anything but boring. People seem to tolerate personal foibles in a national leader if he/she excels in charisma. (In the interest of balance, President Jimmy Carter, whom I admire, is a good man, but he lacks charisma.)

In all the fields referenced above, persons were endowed with natural talents, intellect, instinct, wit, courage, and insight augmented by charisma, fueling unusual achievement. By any measure, even in the absence of the term these persons were archetypes of the "go big" philosophy.

Admittedly, my listing of national figures endowed with charisma represents a subjective judgment. You can and should reflect upon those who shaped the national and global discussion of achievement in diverse fields.

12) Hopes and Helps for the Charisma-challenged

At the same time, we must acknowledge a sad reality in life: some are, charitably, charisma-challenged. That is, they are pedestrian, dull, boring, and unable to persuade people beyond the norm. Indeed, such persons may be nice and kind, but with limited vision, they do not recognize a sense of "go big" in themselves, nor do they celebrate it in others.

Regrettably, as would-be leaders they relish safety, security, the status quo, being accepted by peers, and resenting and resisting new ideas, concepts, and notions. The familiar suits them just fine. I pray you are not of this class of people, for if you are, know that nothing monumental in life or history has ever or will ever be accomplished without some "pizzazz," some display of charisma.

In the view of some, you either have charisma or you don't. Indeed, there is no store wherein you can purchase it. Nor can you read enough, study enough, or research enough concerning charisma in order to gain it. Yet, in some ways it can be cultivated if there is a spark of it in you.

That spark of desire for more, for the "go big," can be enhanced and can deepen latent charisma as you strive for professionalism, punctuality, presence, and profundity. A leader grows through tapping those with skills the leader does not possess. In building a team, each member brings his/her best traits. Thus, by design the charisma-challenged should engage with others who exude charisma. Introverts might well build a team of extroverts.

Another suggestion for the charisma-challenged: allow someone close to you to reveal your strengths and your weaknesses. If you are predictable, a bit boring, or uninspiring, find those traits that are positive: reliable, exhibiting integrity, steady, and more.

If you are insecure, unfortunately, you will be intimidated by those who are charismatic, causing you to flee to your comfort zone.

13) When Creativity and Charisma Meet

Finally, if you relish the "go big" mentality, it requires the combination of creativity and charisma. Some way, somehow, at some point, you must harness new attitudes, new skills, and new objectives, employing them in unique patterns so as to enhance behavior consistent with high achievement.

When this mentality takes precedence, you will encounter unusual opportunities precisely because you expect such to happen in your life. Daily, you await situations that will draw you closer to your stated objectives.

My best advice for those with an inkling of the "go big" mentality is this: accept that you are different, unique, special, born to succeed, and positioned for more in life. Perhaps for some, this realization may be difficult to process intellectually, viscerally, and volitionally. Find your voice, your security, in rigorous self-assessment.

I repeat: Note your SWOT (strengths, weaknesses, obstacles, threats). As family and friends provide unfiltered evaluations of you, they invest in your success. Now you have an accountability group with whom you may chart out your destiny. Also, your regularly meeting with movers and shakers enhances your capacity for achievement. As a sentient creature, you must recognize that others are attaining lofty objectives. Ask yourself, "When will my day come?"

14) Challenges for Leaders

Leaders and high achievers, therefore, must combine several traits: focus, internal motivation, courage, knowledge, strength, optimism, enthusiasm, and risk taking combined with consummate communication skills. All of these traits represent useful tools in your achievement toolbox. Finally, noteworthy success emerges from imaginative reasoning. These achievers are usually ill-suited to maintain the status quo, but wholly dedicated to the pursuit of greater things. I heartily invite you to those ranks.

15) Christians Should Heartily Embrace the "Go Big" Theme

What I strongly advocate as a prod for better aspiration and accomplishment ("go big") strikes many Christians as antithetical to biblical principles of humility. I concede the point. Indeed, we must strive for a proper balance between aspiration and being humble before God. Yet, in His economy there is a place for striving as long as when success comes, we direct praise to God. True success, then, advances His kingdom imperative in Jesus Christ.

In other words, with Christ, Christians have the greatest motivation to succeed. You should consider His soaring admonition: "I came that they may have life, and have *it* abundantly" (John 10:10b). Such "life" encompasses your relationship with God, your relationships with others, your career, and your objectives, all with a better quality of life irrespective of material benefits.

Relative to having "more," I constantly remind our church family that the purpose of abundance should mean the extension of God's kingdom as we, individually and collectively, make tangible contributions to others in the name of our Savior. Accordingly, I pray we will always generate sufficient revenue to evangelize the lost, provide materials for teaching/discipleship, maintain our facilities, compensate staff, strengthen ministries, and collaborate in community outreach while aiding external programs and people, especially those in obvious need.

When Christian congregations help the vulnerable, the broken, and the poor, along with all those facing life's headwinds, we prepare the soil of their hearts for hearing and heeding the Gospel of Jesus Christ: "If a brother or sister is without clothing and in need of daily food, and one of you says to them, 'Go in peace, be warmed and be filled,' and yet you do not give them what is necessary for *their* body, what use is that? Even so faith, if it has no works, is dead, *being* by itself" (James 2:15-17).

Now, aided by a sense of the importance of creativity and charisma in the formulation of high aspiration and high achievement fostering "go big," you should note the synergism when combining these concepts. Most often, successful people are those who properly integrate both in a well-developed life plan. For all who seem to be accidental successes, I would venture that the overwhelming majority have assiduously worked from some well-developed plan, even if it is unarticulated.

CHAPTER 12

Go Big: Patience and Persistence

Conceptually, each chapter builds on everything expressed in previous ones. Accordingly, I want to introduce two more ingredients in producing a principled and pragmatic basis for "go big" achievement.

Good, wholesome, moral, ethical, and lasting success is the product of the alchemy of patience and persistence. Achievers of every stripe harness themselves to a clear goal while patiently and persistently pursuing it until the end. The whole purpose of this book is to add you to the ranks of the successful.

1) Patience Produces Lasting Achievement

While I am cautious in receiving and following advice from those unable to clearly articulate their view of God, informing us how we can come to a saving relationship with Him, I acknowledge the value of evaluating suggested routes to success, especially from those who have, objectively, attained some measure of it.

Without maligning her character, as I do not personally know her, I place Ms. Oprah Winfrey in the category of those confused as to what constitutes true spirituality. Often, I have heard representations alluding to "nature," "spirit," or "the universe" rather than "Jesus Christ" as the way to God the heavenly Father.

Please hear me: many in American culture are not bad, per se; they are just a bit confused in an area that is quite clear—spirituality is based only in Christ. (Yes, that's old-school talk; but it is biblical!)

Admittedly, Ms. Winfrey represents a formidable African-American marketing presence, global icon, and tremendous talent with incredible business acumen. Irrefutably, she is keen to demographics, well-versed in mass tastes, and serves as a mentor and model for striving and achieving in varied aspects of communications, business, and entertainment.

At the same time, I am unmoved by talk shows (and some books!) that supposedly serve as means of empowerment. (Call me cynical and jaded, but many of their viewers and readers choose to remain in toxic relationships, continually make poor choices, remain locked in dead-end employment, fail to embrace education, and fall farther behind every day; yet they celebrate enlightenment devoid of Jesus Christ.)

Equally impressive, this black billionaire commands the respect of millions nationally and globally. Her well-known philanthropy continually stirs my interest, as she possesses the power to literally "make" new authors, products, travel sites, and trends. Indeed, I applaud her school for girls in South Africa (though we need twenty private college-preparatory ones in urban America).

Arguably, she has a singular ability to focus America's attention on any subject she pleases. Some argue her imprimatur helped elect America's first black president! Her wide media exposure includes a wide range of roles: actress, activist, movie producer, magazine editor, book promoter, and life coach. I am enthralled by her Oprah Winfrey Network (OWN) television presence. Her *Life Class* features celebrities, writers, professors, pundits, and national figures sharing critical keys to success.

Yet, we know of Ms. Winfrey now without discerning her patient trek from local newscaster (starting in Nashville, Tennessee, moving on from there to Chicago and on to national syndication) all the way to global influence. Her story is one of long preparation touched by the grace of God. Arguably, today it would prove almost impossible for a young black journalism student to chart out a similar path to worldwide renown.

Over the years in numerous interviews, Ms. Winfrey has shared tough moments in her journey: childhood abuse, dysfunctional family life, weight struggles, racism, and more. Indeed, patient endurance has made her climb to the summit of material success all the more gratifying. Most of all, the arc of her life epitomizes patience in the sense of proper alignment of preparation and opportunity.

2) Within a Life of Patience, There Are Formidable Challenges

Recently, one of Ms. Winfrey's *Life Class* episodes prominently featured comedian/actor/author/talk-show host/entrepreneur Steve Harvey. He told of his eventful professional journey, replete with early career moves, homelessness, success, bankruptcy, divorce, suffering, betrayal, and more. All of these, he stated, over a thirty-year career, were critical to ensuring present achievement. Again, you should note the theme of patience. Nothing good or lasting will come to you without patience. As his career attests, detailed in several books, the combination of patience and persistence will, in the long run, prove quite productive.

As we have done throughout this book, we need to define our terms.

3) Defining Patience, after Its Description

"Patience" references bearing misfortune or pain without complaint; the capacity for being patient (during a delay of uncertain duration); calmly tolerating provocation or delay. It also points to perseverance or diligence, with respect to details. It represents an internal quality and character trait designed to produce lasting results.

From long ago, I learned that patience is a virtue. Now, since that time, I must admit, I have sought to fully examine its meaning. Everybody seems to laud the patient person, even as impatience in America overwhelms so many. I will go even further: at this mature age (presently mid-fifties), I am still grappling with the application of patience to the mundane things of life.

While it is quite advisable to wait for the perfect moment to speak up or engage in action, I still sometimes get it wrong as to when that time is. I am sure I have missed some tremendous benefits because I convinced myself that it would be better to wait for a better time.

As I seek to adopt the appropriate response to all of life, I live a supernatural experience, within the confines of natural existence. In other words, I aim to view life through glorifying God within the prism of His revealed Word, with Jesus Christ as its culmination.

4) Patience as a Biblical Principle

Accordingly, the Bible stresses the importance of patience: "Love is patient. . . ." (1 Corinthians 13:4a). Or, "Therefore be patient, brethren, until the coming of the Lord. The farmer waits for the precious produce of the soil, being patient about it, until it gets the early and late rains. You too be patient; strengthen your hearts, for the coming of the Lord is near" (James 5:7-8). Or, "The Lord is not slow about His promise, as some count slowness, but is patient toward you, not wishing for any to perish but for all to come to repentance" (2 Peter 3:9).

The total revelation from God reminds saints of God's perspective on patience, preserving us by His grace, love, and watchfulness of our condition. Like the farmer, when you deposit the seed into the soil you must wait patiently for the soil to deliver its bounty. This agrarian process cannot be hurried; yet it is always on time. At the same time, God yields His benefits to you in a fashion that He best designs, directs, and determines.

Yet, in capturing this "go big" thesis, I am coming to understand that often you just have to "go for it" without full assurance of every item on your "careful" list. Faith in God does not guarantee perfectly determining the exact moment for a course of action. If it did, Christians would never suffer doubt, pain, sorrow, or regret.

Patience, further, represents a significant virtue in the human spirit, helping you maintain focus on an important objective while inevitable delays inhibit your progress. Tough, challenging, and dark days inform a journey connected to the ultimate Source. In order to navigate these challenges, you need patience.

5) The "Work" of Patience

In no way do I equate patience with passivity, encouraging you to do nothing beyond waiting for achievement to somehow engulf your efforts. Waiting alone, nor hoping alone, nor talking alone will hasten change for the better. Rather, patience continually analyzes its goals, fortifies its substance, and polishes its content while moving toward a quality end. For a Christian, you must sincerely pray, asking God to reveal the acceptable moment of action. You might also seek scriptural principles, linking your life to others in similar situations. Never move, however, until God indicates. And when He indicates, push human reasoning aside and act courageously!

As it all coalesces, patience places you in an unusual place—between enthusiasm and trepidation. Neither of these emotions should be confused with reluctance or ambivalence. You anticipate uncertainty, even as it fills you with a sense of the full range of challenges on the road to the "go big" target you have set for tangible accomplishment.

6) Never Allow Internal, Nagging Questions to Thwart Progress

When you thoroughly analyze any undertaking, it presents intriguing possibilities: What if your desire turns out worse than your present reality? What if you fail in your attempt? What if promised allies fail to materialize? What if the danger you envision actually happens? Who can you turn to if the plan fizzles before your eyes? Might a chorus of "I told you so"s rain down on you?

Amid the definite and the indefinite, there is always that which is ominous. Thus, in many cases it is the prudent course to simply exercise patience. On the other hand, life does not allow for endless analysis. At some point, then, making no decision becomes a decision.

Admittedly, I am torn by the knowledge that patience is necessary, while innumerable benefits are gained by those who refuse to wait. Indeed, over the years I have advised persons of the importance of timing. You should exercise patience until the perfect timing.

For example, no immature, insecure, frivolous couple should marry unless and until each person understands the nature of the covenant and commitment into which her or she is entering. The marriage manual that I for three decades and countless Christian clergy have used for over a century holds that "A union embodying such ideals (love, humility, devotion, fidelity, permanence, godliness, mutual submission, and more) is not to be entered into lightly or unadvisedly, but reverently, discreetly, soberly, and in the fear of God. Into such a union you now come to be joined."

How much heartache, frustration, shame, anger, and loneliness could be avoided if persons would patiently wait for a God-ordained relationship rather than accepting the first proposal that comes along from a dubious suitor? It may, again, sound like a voice from another era: "What explains the rush to marry?" In fact, sound judgment requires prayer, time, reflection, evaluation, and counsel, all indicative of yearning for the leading of God.

As I write these words, a young couple has sought my counsel regarding a possible relocation to our area of the U.S. They are both professionals in the field of education. God's grace has converged with their pursuits. I feel a special closeness to them. While every decision has its share of trepidation, as they explained the matter to me, I blurted out, "This is the best news I've heard all day. You need to hurry, sell that house, and move back home to KC. I don't really understand your hesitance."

Please, reader, hear my heart. Absolutely, you must pray to God for guidance. Yet, once you commit the matter to Him you then must consult a few spiritual sources (for divine confirmation). Once you receive peace regarding the petition before God, you should then engage in action. Then, stop obsessing over whether it is right or the right time. Rather, faith in God often requires a trusting leap into His arms!

7) Examining "Impatient Patience"

So perhaps some resolution comes from a hybrid concept, one that might seem contradictory: "impatient patience." That is, accept the need for patience as inescapable, as some matters lie outside your realm of control. However, knowing that you cannot bring a matter to fruition must not mean acceptance of a negative scenario. Maybe an illustration can help make my case.

If obtaining a bachelor's degree from an accredited, prestigious, well-regarded academic institution usually takes four years, patience would advise taking and mastering the courses required in the curriculum. Then, await the elapsing of four years. The "impatient" addendum to "patience" might mean making sacrifices (longer periods of study, few extracurricular activities, taking available summer courses) so as to hasten your progress toward the goal of a degree in a timely manner. In the process, you may discover that because of your intense focus, you reached your objective earlier than you anticipated. In some cases, you might graduate early. In others, you can begin planning for a professional career a bit earlier than the normal student-graduate.

The "impatient patience" that I describe suggests my general philosophical bent: persistence characterizes those captured by the "go big" notion.

8) Defining Persistence

Persistence references the strong, focused, driving ambition to remain with a project, idea, notion, or objective, irrespective of the stress, strain, or struggle involved. Successful living pivots on the degree to which you embrace persistence amid all you must face. Persistence represents the steady, ever-stronger knock at a closed door, knowing that this door will only open from the courage to confront, along with prevailing power by a dogged pursuer.

In an unusual sense, persistence means to continue steadfastly or often annoyingly, especially in spite of opposition; to endure tenaciously. In other words, in order to "go big," anticipating naysayers, you need bulldog tenacity to sustain you through trials, tests, and temptations, alluring you to give up your aspiration.

While it seems simplistic and axiomatic, it bears repeating: daily living resembles a protracted battle fought on uneven terrain, with the enemy employing guerrilla tactics, using heavy weapons, with the surety of human casualties. Yet, victory can be yours, provided you commit to persistence.

9) National Inability to Persist

As I listen to news broadcasts, talk shows, reality television, and the drama of social media, America has become a nation of excuse makers, wimps, wusses, and crybabies. Individually and collectively, too many seem to have lost the persistence gene. One challenge (long-ago abuse) is enough to set you back indefinitely. Two challenges (animosity or vile speech) set in motion your knee-jerk victimization mechanism. And, conveniently, there are organizations, spokespersons, and other enablers to aid pitiful causes.

Nationally, our fixation on the "now" inhibits reflection, articulation of principles, developing a coherent strategy, and alignment of tactics, all for a prolonged campaign to register a significant victory. So you plod along, the victim of circumstances.

This "now" fixation, rash orientation writ large in American culture may prevent you from desiring or procuring quality education (need to quickly work, make money—often, even if it amounts to menial, minimum-wage employment). Some good counsel: employment should be pursued on the basis of a "fit"; do you really belong in this corporate environment, non-profit, or small-business environment? Eight to ten hours a day in a milieu you hate represents a waste of precious time and energy!

Or, you may have trouble forming healthy relationships (can't wait for Mr. or Ms. Right; instead, you settle for Mr. or Ms. "Right now"). The choice of and commitment to a life partner should not be the result of age, boredom, envy, or a desire for just "someone." Some more good counsel: "It's always better to await God's specific choice for you!"

Or, you may fail to discover God's best plan for your life (salvation, integrity, dedication, valor, loyalty, morality). The best counsel: No life is complete devoid of God at its core.

10) Real, Wise, Dynamic Leaders Champion Persistence

Today, the leader I seek to follow will operate in a "go big" tradition formed by spirituality, substance, and style. Accordingly, he will prayerfully reflect on an action, visualize its end, marshal pertinent facts, articulate the best methods, work in confident composure, epitomize decency and dignity, and maintain focus on his course while keeping all involved apprised as to the ongoing viability of the venture. Such a leader will push you when necessary and comfort you along your journey. When your enthusiasm wanes, you need a leader's persistence to bring concept to fruition.

Unstable, vacillating, spineless leaders, especially illustrated in lack of persistence, signal the death-blow for otherwise successful undertakings. In a careful, wise, comforting yet provoking manner, leaders lead by persistence.

Our families, communities, states, nation, and world have lost precious ground as leaders seem to register rather than regulate the temperature of the times. Those to whom we look for wisdom and guidance seem just as confused as everyone else.

In humility, God has given me tremendous leadership opportunities—from a youth to a young minister/pastor to a middle-aged leader—spanning a half-century of life. In every case, He has shown me the value of persistence. Or, as a cherished buddy says to me: "Hang in there, boy!"

11) Lacking Core Values like Persistence, Culture Faces Multiple Crises

In politics, opinion polls drive decision making. In academia, political correctness rules to the point of insanity. In homes, the absence of strong, godly fathers force single mothers to do all within their powers to set high standards, reliable rules, moral values, and social skills while providing for families on one income. During challenging economic times, these mothers often consider moral compromise. A word of wisdom to single mothers: Never put a new man ahead of your children. Don't compromise your morals!

In local communities, vocal minorities dominate the discussion with dubious grievances. In various Christian congregations, obstinate voices drown out the Word, refute Christ's will, ignore the Spirit's direction, flout godly vision, and ignore the kingdom of God's agenda, amid cowering, confused pastors. In larger Christian organizations influenced by narcissism, loss of mission/purpose has hastened concomitant dissipation of constituent enthusiasm, finances, and support. In their wake, vaunted institutions deteriorate.

What I yearn for in life is relatively simple: wise persistence in leaders, like a cruise ship captain taking passengers on an adventure of a lifetime, moving through choppy waters without the acquiescence of all aboard. Small agendas devoid of persistence by those leading large organizations will never achieve grand objectives. So I appeal for persistent, visionary, bold, dynamic leaders. Will you pray with me for the same?

Some ideas are quite self-evident; if significant and lasting achievement were easy or simple, someone would have achieved in that area long ago. For example, until inventor Thomas Edison brought together the unprecedented properties of the light bulb, millions groped in semi-darkness. Yet, interestingly, Edison did not initially succeed as an inventor. The fact is, he discovered ninety-nine ways to fail, right before the hundredth try brought success!

What, we might ask, kept Edison going, and what will sustain you along your journey toward the "go big" ideal? It comes down to that wonderful combination of patience and persistence. Patience represents the capacity to see the long-term view, while persistence aids along a somewhat arduous journey.

In many cases, lacking evidence, patience pushes you to encourage yourself, as many surrounding you have doubt. At the same time, persistence also "talks" to the achiever: "Man, this is nothing! You've been through much worse. At the end of this month, it will be infinitely better. Hold on to your faith and confidence."

For the maturing in Christ, my advice is compelling: Remind yourself of the unfulfilled promises of God. Indeed, "Greater is He who is in you than he who is in the world" (1 John 4:4b).

CHAPTER 13

Go Big: Processing Change

In your quest to make an indelible mark in life, an aspect of the "go big" objective, you need to quickly acquaint yourself with processing change. Truly, change proves difficult for many to envision. Change moves you from comfort to confusion to chaos and, all too often, to conflict.

Change challenges conventional wisdom, sacred cows, established norms, worn-out tradition, and more. It calls for reorientation in your routine. It reshapes the realm of the possible, challenging you to think and to act differently. Change, though often difficult, is absolutely necessary for progress.

Dinosaurs became extinct despite their size, dominance, and sway over other life forms. Ultimately, they were unable to instinctually process or manage change, which requires nimbleness and adaptability to new circumstances. After centuries of dominance, dinosaurs were outwitted and outmaneuvered by smaller, agile, and cunning animals. The dinosaur's heft could not sustain him any longer.

In similar ways, you dare not fall into certain patterns of conceptualization which, if not altered, will ensnare you in limited thinking, resulting in few options or limitations in other indices of possibilities toward sustained success.

In processing change, you need the integration of idea, insight, and inspiration filtering through individuals, and dominating institutions. That is an essential attribute if you expect to maintain the "go big" philosophy over time.

A simple conversation one day with a Christian colleague revealed the degree to which people are afraid of change. Here's how it unfolded: We commiserated over a poorly supported, dying, longtime, lethargic scenario. Also, nearly everyone involved agreed it needed change. When I restated the problem and my proposal for change, he replied, "Man, that's true, and it does needs changing; but it's a hornet's nest. Good luck changing that one."

Processing change occasions such challenges. Think of it: You feel badly concerning a negative thing; you have the intellectual tools for change; you sense its change will benefit the greater good. In the end, you remain in a situation not conducive to good health or happiness. At the same time, others allow the condition to repeat itself. Why? Perhaps a few considerations will aid our inquiry.

1) Change Requires Courage over Comfort

In the New Testament, a small band of would-be activists led by the ultimate "go big" agent, Jesus Christ, are instrumental in transforming the world. They adhere to a revolutionary ethic of love for God, leading to the advancement of His kingdom centered in embracing the unique Christ as Savior. Among this band, we are continually drawn to the exploits of one, Simon Peter.

Peter distinguishes himself from the others, expressing himself in ways that are rash, profane, earthy, quick-witted, and assertive. Able to quickly appraise a matter without always plumbing its depths, I appreciate Peter's desire and action orientation, signaling a restive nature.

Change, most often, is fostered by such personality types, such "misfits." Extroverts like Peter shape destiny, while introverts (Am I speaking to you?) obsess over the crowd's comfort.

For some, change-oriented courage is more admired than emulated. After some time, you can no longer contentedly watch the parade of history pass you by. Restive in spirit, you must participate in it. For you, it is far easier to actually jump from an airborne plane than to describe skydiving while on land. Sadly, for a few, safety on the ground supplants soaring in the air.

To really "go big," you must resist the temptation to take the road well traveled over against the less-traveled one. Well-worn by time and circumstance, some blithely follow previous travelers.

Peter, however, casts aside comfort, grabs opportunity by the lapels and seizes the moment, all while optimizing his moment to shine. Please consider a riveting example of Peter's assertive complex, depicted in Matthew 14:25-30. The best portion of that text, for our purposes, involves verses 28 and 29: "Peter said to Him, 'Lord, if it is You, command me to come to You on the water.' And He said, 'Come!' And

Peter got out of the boat, and walked on the water and came toward Jesus."

In this moment, Peter's life is forever changed. At Peter's inquiry, the power of Christ issues an astounding command. It represents a command of mammoth proportions. While I certainly thank God in Christ for exerted authority over the atmosphere (here, water), I also celebrate Peter's willingness to defy logic, rationality, laws of physics, and more in a greater pursuit. That pursuit involves Peter's coming to the Master, with the water serving as the greatest hindrance to its fulfillment. So Peter achieves a supernatural "go big": he walks on the water!

Peter's request for permission to get out of the boat needs to be thoroughly analyzed, as it offers rich insight for those aiming to achieve at the highest levels: "Lord, if it is You, command me to come to You on the water." In effect, Peter requests a summons to grand attainment.

Within the context of this Scripture passage, I am amazed at the unfolding tableau: twelve of Christ's disciples see the same phenomenon (Christ walking on the water), hear the same summons from Him ("Come!") which ignites their possible enlarged capacity, yet only Peter enjoys the "go big" experience.

While the focus rightly shines on Peter, you need to ask, "Why didn't the other disciples, at the very least, try to walk on the water?"

Of course, we can only engage in conjecture, but it seems reasonable that the disciples relied more on the laws of physics (water cannot support the weight of upright creatures) than on the power of God (if He invites persons to walk on water, He makes it possible!). So they remained comfortable in the boat, shielded from danger.

Yet in this case, Christ's disciples are also unable to bask in utter exhilaration, joyful abandonment, and incredible triumph, such as Peter experiences momentarily while walking on the water. In the telling of the sages of African-American preaching, Peter walks on the water, strong and confident, like a man walking on pavement. That imagery engenders greater honor for the Master, more so than for the man Peter.

Further, in my imagination some of Christ's other disciples who chose not to leave the boat sat there smug, dry, and satisfied. Peter, after being on the water, sees the wind. Thus, he sinks into the water. Now drenched, Peter calls for the Lord to save him. Human nature being fixed, his companions may have chided him for the temerity of trying to walk on the water: "Peter, look at you, wet due to hubris. Whereas, look at us, dry because of our fears." In that imagined scenario, I strongly identify with Peter. I hope you can as well. Indeed, it is far better to get wet as you attempt something unusual than to remain dry while embracing the mundane, for life represents a daily adventure.

Shifting the focus to the boat, it symbolizes a small physical sphere from which Peter seeks an exit. Their imperiled boat proves too dull and boring for the impetuous disciple. In a related way, Theodore Roosevelt said, "Far better it is to dare mighty things than to rank with the poor spirits who neither suffer much nor enjoy much because they live in the gray twilight." Instead, Peter seeks the limitless Christ, whom he can only reach by going on the water.

In Jesus Christ, we see the one who transcends spherical and psychological limitations. Christ has the infinite capacity to move His own toward a larger vista. Thus, His reaching them on the water here in Matthew 14 in the "fourth watch of the night" illustrates Christ's limitless possibilities. His buoyancy on the water transfers to those in spiritual relationship with Him for the glory of God.

The last rationale for Peter's leaving the boat and walking on the water represents getting beyond the stifling confines of his comrades, the faithless disciples, who remain comfortable in the boat. Often, you may be stymied from the "go big" ideal because of the company you keep. Those of low self-esteem, given to mediocrity while satisfied with minimal, unable to see beyond a setback, cannot be expected to cheer you on to victory. And if such persons knew the surest route, they would have taken it long ago! Thus, you need to "get out of the boat"!

- Get out of the boat of the silly, ignorant, dumb, and foolish.
- Get out of the boat of limited vistas.
- Get out of the boat of limited perspective.
- Get out of the boat of low self-regard.
- Get out of the boat of laziness.

- Get out of the boat of envy and jealousy.
- Get out of the boat of past hurts, abuse, or setback.

Once out of those "boats," the scenery becomes much brighter! And you start recognizing "go big" possibilities. You start seeing yourself in new places, enjoying new opportunities in the company of new colleagues. Please note a fresh revelation. Recently, a friend took his wife to Dubai for vacation. They thoroughly enjoyed it. He called it a "seven-star" experience. To my knowledge, he is among a small group of black preachers/wives to have the Dubai experience. Now, I am inspired to change my routine: I must take my wife there, or some other exotic destination! This point leads to the next one.

2) Change Requires an Alluring Idea

Just as Peter lived by a transcendent idea, throughout history ideas have fueled attempts that, if proven successful, are then judged "great." People usually include in the "great" idea category a range of advances: aviation, telephones, automobiles, dams, bridges, ferries, railroads, cures for diseases, space exploration, computers, Internet, social media, and millions more.

These ideas drive inventors to their shops, keeping them up late, fueling their passion for new techniques, products, and services to optimize conveniences and increase options that make the world better. When they succeed, bringing forth a new discovery, it immeasurably enhances humankind.

Further, these notions prompt scientists and researchers to their labs, probing, questioning dogma, wondering "What if . . . ?" All of these attempts push the parameters of the knowable, opening new areas of insight for the betterment of humanity.

Indeed, epic, sweeping, compelling ideas often come to those willing to question the stated, accepted, and prevailing order. Inevitably, your questions will offend some while inspiring others. As an experienced Christian leader, I have learned that many want to raise the unsaid, but they are hesitant, fearing entrenched interests. Early on in Christian ministry, I was hesitant regarding exerting myself as a leader. Now, if I am convinced the matter is just, right, and timely, I have the responsibility to state it. I encourage you to grow into the leadership paradigm. For me, in the Old Testament prophetic tradition, under God, honoring Jesus Christ, guided by God's Holy Spirit, I leave it to the group to determine if my suggestion should prevail.

Also, like the Old Testament prophets, some ideas await the proper time. While I accept the wisdom of timing, particularly God's timing, in faith I stand ready to move in a progressive fashion. Right now!

Allured by a consuming, unusual, divine idea, I don't understand your reticence. Once you discover God's leading, every moment you hesitate represents a moment you have wasted, one which proves difficult to retrieve.

3) Change Reflects Insight

When you endeavor toward a significant milestone in life, change must serve as your preferred vehicle. Within a framework of achievement, you discover unusual insight. Changes in mind should in some way connect with changes in outlook, fortitude, and behavior. With heightened sensitivity into the matter, you will realize the need for change. It proves difficult, if not impossible, to remain moored to a mode of operation once you have seen and embraced something different and better.

The great benefit of increased exposure, for example, is its ability to expand your knowledge, which fosters change. People reared in rural, insular settings often embrace change in wardrobe, hair, dental work, speech patterns, dietary choices, and network of friends while hopefully raising their aspirations. What is the fuel for the changes? In many instances, these persons have taken a trip to a teeming urban setting. There, they have seen more, experienced more, and connected with a more diverse populace. Clearly, it is possible to rebel against "high-falutin'" ways. Yet, in the main, I have seen the positive effects of wider exposure and deeper insights.

Born in the city of angels, Los Angeles, reared near the bright, alluring lights of Hollywood, I have actual and anecdotal evidence of those who repudiated native places of birth, searching for fulfillment, fame, and fortune as, for example, an acclaimed entertainer. Within six months of arrival there, small-town values have been supplanted, with many becoming enamored with and corrupted by the speed and seduction of the big city. Of course, this vignette represents the negative side of wider exposure.

On the positive side, tremendous opportunities for insight, enlightenment, and growth await you when you change your locale. Without denigrating whole regions of America or those who find peace and tranquility there, I am fully advocating the inherent benefits of change. Dumb, stale, uninspiring traditions often thrive in the swamp of small-town settings, with natives fearful of outsiders who seem disrespectful of mores, folkways, and rhythms of life there.

That insular atmosphere reminds me of a real-life story shared by a friend. In the mid-1930s, he had been born. He was then reared in a small town, with the requisite large water tower, with a posted population of 967 citizens. He declared upon high school graduation, his fervent prayer, driving ambition, and utmost objective: change that town's population to 966 by personally leaving town!

After he did so, he became one of America's finest African-American expository preachers, Rev. Dr. A. Louis Patterson Jr. of Houston, Texas (referenced earlier). Most who knew him and heard him lift the name of Christ affirm the change of place did him—and the world—quite well!

4) Whether Change Occurs Gradually or Spontaneously, You Bow to It

In life, you quickly reach the conclusion that change is inevitable. In fact, the only constant in the world is rapid change. For example, seasons change; hairstyles change; minds change; city skylines change; prices change. Unfortunately, and increasingly, even values and accepted norms change! Make no mistake that biblical or Christocentric ones do not change, but the way many perceive them does.

Things change in other ways as well. Consider that new store on the corner. Six months ago, the site was a car wash. Or that road was clogged for so long: now, the traffic flows after they changed it by widening it. Or consider that spanking-new housing complex which replaced an eyesore. We should all be glad for that! Or think of that new office holder, elected three months ago, replacing an entrenched politician. Once in office, we sincerely hope the new one keeps campaign promises.

These changes range from the trivial to the critical. Yet, if you are alive and alert, you are engulfed in the changes occurring all around. Some changes resemble a tsunami, wreaking devastation in its wake. Other changes resemble a gentle breeze, subtle in its approach, changing the landscape in ways that are at first imperceptible. Either way, you are obliged to acquiesce to change, as it becomes inevitable.

5) Change Produces Anticipation of a Fresh Approach

In processing change, you must embrace the necessity of a fresh approach. For example, within a home, among many challenges over time, you will find it necessary to replace the roof, reconfigure the landscape, paint the walls, buy new furniture, install new lighting, purchase new appliances, or replace carpeting. All of these are indicators of change necessary in the progression of life.

In professional life also, processing change is a constant. After many years, worksites move, new coworkers are integrated, rebranding (different company name, logo, and motto) occurs, managers are hired, and new CEOS are brought aboard while new policies are promulgated. When people, practices, products, and processes are brought together, the culture of the entity is changed. As companies expand their national footprint, "outsourcing," "downsizing," and "right-sizing" gain traction as corporate-speak, signaling massive changes in the offing. Also, acquisitions of smaller companies and mergers will change the overall environment. If that were not enough, job descriptions expand amid myriad changes you may be called upon to process.

Indeed, the workday becomes increasingly hectic as the commute may become longer, fraying nerves in the process. In this scenario, the work-life balance gets thrown out of whack. No wonder, then, that workplace violence incidents make news across America. Those overstressed without outlets (sufficient downtime, exercise, diversions, or spiritual resources) may succumb to mounting psychological pressure.

Knowing these daily realities in the workplace, you must prepare yourself for change. Here is a strategy for processing change.

6) Assess Your Adaptability to Change

In the aforementioned workplace example, adaptability to change would encompass celebrating, first, having the gift of life, health, and strength. Second, maintain gratitude to God for stable employment. Third, embrace the new site, coworkers, policies, and supervisors as components of a fresh start. Fourth, tap into your creativity, adorning your desk or cubicle with pictures of family members, favorite team paraphernalia, memos to self, comics, vacation souvenirs, and more. During the workday, no matter the stressors, you have pieces of life to reflect upon, reminding you of your love connections. Indeed, while work proves essential for financial wherewithal, family and friends serve as emotional shock absorbers for all that you must face.

Add to that, for those committed to God through Jesus Christ, you can rely upon spiritual resources (worship, prayer, the Bible, small groups, Christian fellowship, books, tapes, music, and more) to strengthen your areas of weakness.

Characteristic of the "go big" mentality is the ability to quickly interpret a new reality while processing all that you will need to do now that the situation has forever changed.

7) What You Must Change, Commit to Doing It

Over the course of nearly forty years of Christian ministry, including counseling and engagement with many people across America, I have found commonality among races, cultures, ethnicities, income disparities, and upbringing whether urban or rural, politically liberal or conservative. Among many, we agree on one thing: people know all the right words to say, the proper vows to make. Yet, after the sessions conclude, some will change through personal work while others remain mired in good intentions. If you really want change, your head, heart, and will must align. Then, through radical intentionality, tenacity, consistency, integrity, and specificity, something real, fundamental, and lasting will result.

Along with the prompting toward change, I would add a note of urgency. The surest route to significant achievement bends toward those ready to engage the task right now!

In the Old Testament record, particularly as the Exodus of the Jews from Egypt appears imminent, Moses offers Pharaoh this advice: "'The honor is yours to tell me: when shall I entreat for you and your servants and your people, that the frogs be destroyed from you and your houses, *that* they may be left only in the Nile?' Then [Pharaoh] said, 'Tomorrow'" (Exodus 8:9-10a).

If this intriguing text had not been included in the Holy Writ, it would seem an insertion by one seeking to make the point of historic evidences of foolish delays. Clearly, had Pharaoh simply requested it, the frogs would have immediately ceased their torment of Pharaoh, his land, and his people. Yet, incredibly, Pharaoh—overwhelmed, uncertain, frustrated, and completely flummoxed—endures another night with the frogs!

Ambivalence, excuses, critics, procrastination, inertia, cynics, hyper-analysis, and self-doubt litter the highway, thwarting those who are serious regarding attainment of an envisioned objective. At the same time, the wheels of inevitable change roll over that same highway. You control whether you will embrace change or rue its steady movement. I hope you will celebrate change as your necessary prompt toward the "go big" life.

8) The Pace of Adaptability References Your Achievement

You may be ready to adapt to a new reality, but change still intimidates many otherwise successful people. Perhaps you will rush toward change if you take a page from corporate thinking. Repeatedly, I am drawn to the marketing genius of the McDonald's Corporation. Several decades ago, they started with a simple beef patty sandwich with condiments. French fries and a soft drink completed the meal.

Later, as consumers became more calorie-conscious, McDonald's switched to an emphasis on salads, among a number of healthy eating options. Aiming to remain relevant in the fast-food industry, McDonald's now offers a dizzying array of dining options, including pork ribs (McRib sandwich), chicken bites (McNuggets), and gourmet coffees (McCafé). Indeed, they have maintained profitability and market share by being sensitive to changes in consumer choices.

Likewise, in any successful venture you must understand current trends, cultural tastes, and resilience to offer your services to those who want and need them. Achievement, then, affirms your ability to adapt quickly to a rapidly changing world.

There is another major industry—computer technology—that envisions, inspires, and then manages change. In the process of product evolution, this industry calls millions to adapt to its multiple usages. Over the last twenty years, the global lexicon has adapted to the technological revolution occurring before our eyes. Personal computers (PCs) have been supplanted by tablets, with smartphones and GPS systems rounding out the slate of innovations.

Somewhere, I heard this wise formulation: "Be careful as the pioneer of change, while avoiding the tendency of being the last to embrace it." So, practically speaking, I covet the newest technological advance, even if I am unfamiliar with all its usages. I figure it is much easier to learn new tasks when I own new tools.

9) Depression Reflects Inability to Manage Change

You do not need a degree in psychology to know that many people, despite smiles on their faces, are suffering under the weight of depression. They betray depression, a blanket of despair, in several ways: negativity in interpersonal relationships, rising addiction to drugs and alcohol, marriage and birthrate declines, while losing confidence in future achievements.

It is little wonder, then, that the depressed quickly fall prey to hucksters, charlatans, motivational speakers, and others who promise to lift sagging spirits for a nominal fee. Society should abhor slick, self-absorbed, success "experts" who, in my view, are quite gifted in separating depressed, vulnerable people from their meager financial resources. After the elaborate hype of a success presentation, many are left in their same condition.

As we analyze the notion of self-help, we note an inherent danger when your thoughts are elevated without a pragmatic plan to achieve at that promised "next level." You have been informed of unprecedented health, wealth, creativity, and positive energy. Then, after several failed attempts, nothing changes! "Believe in yourself," "reach for the stars," and "celebrate your future" are wonderful exhortations, but they need an attached action plan for implementation.

10) Change Proves Difficult because It Repudiates Entrenched Thinking

Again, even without an advanced degree in psychology, without a psychiatric practice, all would agree that ingrained patterns of behavior are difficult to break. You may know that from painful reflections on your own mistakes and lapses of good judgment. If only people could thoroughly consider the long-term consequences of their actions prior to engaging in them. That's where adaptability to change enters your scenario.

Real change means you tire of conducting your life's business in the same manner, hoping for incredible results. Lacking color, personality, panache, style, swagger, and "sizzle," you may find life tedious and boring. Someway, however, you must embrace change as a necessary ally in your ascension in the "go big" life you dream of.

As a transplant to America's Midwest, I have come to understand change from the perspective of the daily weather. Almost year-round, I know that the weather can change without overt warning. The day may begin sunny, bright, and fair. Yet, before evening ominous clouds arrive, darkening the sky and turning it into torrential showers. (Accordingly, I plan for weather changes, with a hat, light coat, and umbrella in my trunk.) If I understand and accept such drastic changes in the weather, I should by all means anticipate and prepare for major changes in my life.

11) Changed People Change the World!

I am fascinated by the trajectory of lives, especially those who started with little but now live in abundance. Recently I asked a millionaire acquaintance to express the spark that fueled his ascent. He described a poor upbringing, albeit with a strong work ethic. Then, he excelled in academic preparation, graduating from an Ivy League institution. From there, he worked for a small company. By all accounts, he should have been happy; inside, however, he was restless.

He sensed that he was not making the difference in life he felt capable of achieving. Taking a major chance, he established a small business in a field in which he felt competent. Early on, revenue was limited, with two other paid employees. After a few years, in consultation with customers and would-be customers, he discovered what his small company was doing wrong. He worked on his strengths, while eliminating his weaknesses. A few years later, a much larger company acquired his small firm, giving him, as sole owner, lifetime economic security.

Today, this young entrepreneur dabbles in many endeavors—business investments, philanthropy, support for political causes/candidates, and more. While he may not yet be known across America, I predict he will have a bright future, making an enormous impact, as he possesses a sharp mind, passion for varied causes, ability to articulate his position, and directness and dedication to the task. In all ways, he epitomizes a formidable change agent.

12) Change Occurs, Ultimately, after a Series of Challenges

New York Governor Andrew Cuomo, experienced political operative and former HUD Secretary in the Clinton administration, extols the virtues of political leadership in a tough environment. After recounting personal pain (past electoral defeats, a highly publicized divorce, and more), he offers a telling commentary on the relationship between politics and the media: "There are very few examples of success that are uninterrupted escalations." On the ladder of success, then, there are broken or missing rungs. To reach the top, you must navigate various obstacles. Indeed, after passing through pain, doubt, frustration, innumerable challenges, and stressful circumstances, you celebrate successful achievement.

In a larger sense, finally, managing change on the way to notable achievement requires that you possess a unique skill set: passion, enthusiasm, grit, "fire in the belly," resilience, stamina, pragmatism, and intensity of engagement. While the process of reaching a high goal might be ugly and distasteful, its product is wonderful. In a word, daily you must relish the game, the fight, the struggle, and the give-and-take while never capitulating to your opponents. They never win until and unless you surrender.

CHAPTER 14

Go Big: Defined by Discipline

It can be proven that nothing substantive will happen for you if not for a life of discipline. Even though they arrive at the "go big" level by different means, legions of achievers affirm the fact that the common denominator in reaching an unusual objective comes down to discipline.

Indeed, in life, since so many discuss discipline, it is necessary to define it. Then you can examine its presence or absence in your daily activities.

1) Defining Discipline

A classic definition of *discipline* views it as training to act in accordance with rules; instruction designed to train to proper conduct or action; the training effect of experience, adversity, and the like. Also, it involves behavior in accord with rules of conduct; a branch of instruction or learning, with a view to action. Further, discipline references punishment in order to train and control.

Further, discipline represents training that develops self-control, character, integrity, orderliness, or efficiency. It involves subjection to rule and submission to authority (self, law, centralized, highest power in the universe). Further, it captures the necessary instruction toward an acceptable outcome.

The negative aspect of discipline involves the correction, chastisement, or punishment inflicted (psychological, physical, financial, relational) as the intended corrective and training toward a desired end.

Good discipline, therefore, involves inculcating values, ideals, and core principles within a regimented course of action. If you rigorously adhered to it, discipline will produce a certain favorable objective.

All of the nuances of discipline detailed above should be analyzed in the quest for lasting achievement.

Let's walk through aspects of these definitions so as to ensure appreciation of all that discipline requires of and from you to become a "go big" achiever. Each item below comprises vital aspects of discipline:

2) Discipline in Daily Action

The main thrust of discipline expects an individual to demonstrate regularity of dedication beyond a mere good start, embodying good continuation, all the way to the point of noticeable results. If your goal involves a hefty savings account, you cannot celebrate with just one $25 deposit. That represents a good start, but if the goal is $500, discipline dictates monthly regularity.

The same holds true for losing twenty pounds. Your attitude, fervor, diet, and exercise regimen must be commensurate with your objective. A little note: some lose twenty pounds only to find thirty new ones!

In the supernatural realm, if the objective involves spiritual maturity, you must not expect fifteen minutes of solitude with God one day out of the week to produce it. Likewise, spiritual intimacy with God will not result from a few moments in Bible study, or once-a-week worship, or occasional tithing. In every case, the goal of going deeper in your relationship with God, like any significant relationship, requires discipline by way of regularity.

In the definition of discipline, you see the "training" aspect, in that it forces you to act in accordance with the aspiration. Athletes must train consistently if they expect to see results on the field, on the court, or in the ring. Actors and actresses must give themselves to training by way of rehearsals (studying their lines, hitting their spots, enunciating properly, learning the ways of others in the cast, following the director's prompts) and more. Often, it can represent a tedious process. Yet, it has a positive effect: ensuring good discipline.

In several fields of achievement, you must apply discipline: military, corporate, academic, professional, relational, and spiritual productivity in advancing the kingdom of God through Jesus Christ.

3) Well-accepted Spheres of Discipline

Soldiers in the military can only expect to achieve higher rank in proportion to the type of discipline they exemplify in the daily exercise of their duties. As they respect the military code, the chain of command, and execute their assigned duties, discipline becomes a standard of judgment.

In the corporate world, performance, professionalism, punctuality, productivity, personality, and working with colleagues and under mentors with extreme discipline inevitably leads to new assignments and greater responsibilities. Your faithful, collegial, timely, and creative exercise of such responsibilities reflects the importance of discipline.

Acclaimed American authors underscore discipline, crafting several chapters each day in order to reach the level of best-selling author. In examining their approach to the craft, they respect the rigors of the routine, perhaps to the point of ritual, affirming a quote from W. H. Auden: "Routine, in an intelligent man, is a sign of ambition."

People who lead ordered, routine, predictable, anal-retentive lives receive a negative appraisal in present-day American culture. (Oh, how I know that!) Yet, life represents a paradox. In situation after situation, a pattern emerges: order and discipline are the catalysts for creativity and daring.

Families need predictability and discipline if children are to feel security in a threatening world. So, too, do local communities, as leaders guide and provide the infrastructure of housing, parks, grocers, roads, bridges, hospitals, police and fire protection, honest judges, and orderly schools. Nations of the world cry out for order, a set of assumed norms and routines that all nations adhere to (United Nations!).

Without discipline in academia, none will advance the proverbial ladder of success. Undergraduates receive baccalaureate credentials then often move into graduate studies, culminating in a doctoral thesis, with full honor as a respected leader in their field. Along the academic path, one constant remains: rigorous dedication to studies. Mastering a tough, diverse, multifaceted, demanding curriculum will position you for the future. Increasingly, academics testify before Congress in shaping important legislation and consult with the executive branch of government. Research by university professors and other acclaimed scholars quite often leads to discoveries, sometimes culminating in Nobel Peace prizes in varied disciplines.

The path to tenured professorship moves according to a recognized discipline: stellar academic credentials, research, publishing papers, books, and more, speaking at conferences, presenting peer-reviewed studies, professionalism, collegiality, and more. Then, one goes before a board of experienced professors as they rigorously assess a candidate's proven potential. Mysteriously, then, one is informed of their judgment. Once tenure is granted, a professor joins the ranks of the esteemed on a college campus. With new research and achievement, he/she immeasurably adds to university life.

In a large, well-regarded law firm, the path to partnership may also be a long one. Increasingly, associates must work well in their fields (polishing their craft, putting in long hours, winning cases, thereby racking up lucrative "billable" hours for the firm). Also, they must bring through the door and then shepherd influential clients through legal entanglements, issues, and challenges. Over some years, they achieve to the point that a managing partner will call them in for a discussion concerning their future with the firm.

At that time, personality, professionalism, productivity, performance, and promise are thoroughly discussed. In the best-case scenario, the outcome will be an offer of partnership, replete with unique status, deference, respect, office space, heightened compensation, and other rarefied perks.

Once you reach your desired level of professional status, it is incumbent that you demonstrate intelligence, team spirit, diligence, enthusiasm, and the ability to handle assigned tasks with unusual dedication, all within the context of daily discipline. More than compensation and benefits alone, valued employees identify with their company as a team member, working toward a shared objective. When the employer-employee relationship really works, the successes of the company become the successes of each worker.

Interpersonal relationships also need the benefit of discipline, in that each person must commit his/her best efforts toward what helps the relationship reach its optimal level. Romantic gestures (cards, calls, gifts, kindnesses) keep alive any special relationship. Such acts, spontaneously, regularly, and within your budget, signal deep affection. Discipline reminds you to maintain fidelity, as well as the initial fervor for the object of your affections.

Cultivation of the fine arts help hone discipline—in music, painting, sculpture, or dance and choreography. Discipline involves the high challenge for those seeking to achieve. Question: Do you really want success? If so, you must exercise discipline.

Musical achievement requires learned qualities; for musicians, this means recognizing, inculcating, and playing the correct notes, while singers must integrate reading notes, rhythm, breathing, coordination, and more. These aspects of musical discipline must be repeatedly practiced. I love this old joke: A young musician, while in a New York City taxicab, asks the driver, "Buddy, how do I get to Carnegie Hall?" The cab driver's response is insightful: "You gotta really practice!"

Painting requires skills that can only be developed through mentoring, training, study, history, appreciation of the masters, theory, and practical engagement. Similarly, sculpture necessitates understanding material compounds, long hours, failure, and quitting thoughts before the benefits of discipline unveil themselves.

Dance and choreography achievement involve dance theory, history, apprenticing with the masters, athleticism, strength, artistry, technique, balance, range of motion, body articulation, dynamics, rehearsals, falls, muscle aches, cramps, awkward twists, hurt feet, bruised egos, temper tantrums, maniacal directors, petty dancers, and more. If you wish to follow in the literal or figurative steps of Balanchine, Baryshnikov, Fosse, Nureyev, or Ailey, you must commit to the discipline of dance.

At the same time, I am troubled by those acclaimed as overnight successes, fearing they will become one-hit wonders rather than persons with a long career, whatever the field of achievement. In developing proficiency in your chosen field, your many years' experience qualify you for multiple tasks. Discipline leads to capacity for long-term success. In fact, equal to other considerations forming previous chapters, you should place discipline as a critical determinant in cultivating the "go big" philosophy.

4) Discipline Transforms "Have To" into "Get To"

Observation and chronological maturity confirm that what you start out ruing as "have to," when adhered to as a regular part of your life, over time becomes "get to." Passionate pursuit (discipline) reaps dividends in the sense of personal privilege.

In other words, rising early to jog in the morning, or walk golf fairways with friends, or read the newspaper, or exercise on home fitness machines starts out as, "Do I have to . . . ?" When the routine is followed, however, after some time, you will relish the joy of action that brings infinite joy, peace, clarity, and serenity. Indeed, you celebrate the sense of wonderment: "Wow, I get to . . . ."

Friends chide me for my near-obsession of seeking solitude to read for hours on end. Ostensibly, they fear that I am missing all the action in life, with this lonely passion. In fact, however, while reading I reside in a state of bliss, traveling to faraway places in my mind. Once there, I experience infinitely more than others who merely traffic in the mundane, the base, the inconsequential.

Add to that, I usually eat the same breakfast: oatmeal or Cream of Wheat, orange juice, and a muffin, five days out of seven. Some call that monotonous; I call it a disciplined daily diet!

Further, I read several newspapers each day. It represents a discipline designed to cultivate new sources of information, data, statistics, references, and allusions to historical figures of renown. This discipline of the mind sharpens cognitive capacities, giving preaching and writing necessary insight, profundity, relevance, freshness, and vibrancy. Without the daily discipline of reading credible sources, many revert to clichés, bromides, simple formulations, borrowed ideas, and more.

If you care to study the lives of those luminaries from various disciplines listed throughout this book, the common denominator for their success involves discipline. The professional athlete learns and internalizes a discipline, allowing him/her to shine when the right moment occurs. Hours spent in the gym, lifting in the weight room, practicing in solitude to the edge of exhaustion far from the crowds, an athlete toils.

Discipline also defines the admired orator. He/she works on the speech, completing many drafts until all the words and phrases soar, for the purpose of persuading the audience. The literal wastebasket, or its computer version, holds those initial drafts, discarded ideas, ill-conceived thoughts, until the "eureka" moment occurs. In some cases, the would-be orator speaks before a mirror, examining posture, intonation, pronunciation, gestures, and more. These are vital aspects of discipline attendant to the artistry of public speaking.

Lest we forget this: the acclaimed entertainer (comedian, actor, singer, artist) hones the craft through rigorous discipline. Timing for a great comedian is not arrived at by accident, nor is the emotional response elicited from an Academy Award-winning thespian, nor does the singer hit the high note, and nor does the beautiful painting emerge except for discipline in all cases.

If to the amateur achievement seems effortless, it is to the credit of one who laboriously expends time, energy, heart, and stamina in the daily ritual of discipline.

There really is no way to overstress the importance of discipline. It represents one of the significant differences between those who achieve, those who "go big," over against those who lack it, the "go home" hordes.

5) Spiritual Discipline Is a Key Component for Growth in Christ

In the formulation of God's kingdom imperative, Jesus Christ is the only way to spiritual fulfillment before God. Additionally, the Bible represents the manual for faith and practice, with the apostle Paul serving as chief professor in the school of Christian faith. His "lectures" in several New Testament references offer the operative notion "living in Christ." Hear his happy refrain:

> Everyone who competes in the games exercises self-control (discipline) in all things. They then *do it* to receive a perishable wreath, but we an imperishable. Therefore I run in such a way, as not without aim; I box in such a way, as not beating the air; but I discipline my body and make it my slave, so that, after I have preached to others, I myself will not be disqualified." (1 Corinthians 9:25-27)

Here, Paul draws on Corinthian readers' knowledge of the Isthmian games, which were held every two years in an area near Corinth. These games allowed athletes to demonstrate speed, strength, agility, nimbleness, versatility, training, and more. Relative to boxing, Paul will not swing wildly, missing his target. Rather, with discipline, he would box in order to win. Then he switches the metaphor to himself: he will dominate himself, in order to gain the victory. In every possible manner, Paul offers the best definition of spiritual discipline.

Spiritual discipline involves much more: daily prayer, Bible study, times of reflection/meditation, regular worship of God, devotion to Christ; adherence to the leading of God's Holy Spirit, obedience to biblical principles in daily applications, humility, sharing of financial substance, attempts to reach the unsaved with the loving, gracious, Christ-centered plan for salvation, tangible concern for the poor, hurting, sad, marginalized, lonely, aged, disabled among us, fighting attacks of the adversary; adopting a positive, healthy, victorious, dynamic, affirming, sanctified lifestyle, and, through all means, advancing the kingdom of God in human hearts, minds, and wills.

So, in concluding the matter of discipline, it is imperative that you understand it, practice it, and evaluate its impact. Faithfulness to discipline will foster the "go big" ethos in you. Two may walk the same path. One will arrive at some degree of achievement, while the other will stop far short of attainment. Their different outcomes will likely be the degree of discipline in the former, as contrasted by its lack in the latter.

Be it great or small, you must commit to the practice of discipline. Faithfully practiced, across many disciplines, its results will astound you!

CHAPTER 15

Go Big: Mentors Matter

Down through history, the aphorism holds sway: "The apple doesn't fall far from the tree." One meaning of the assertion is that somewhere along the line, a successful person has undoubtedly been mentored by another successful person. Long ago, in marital relations when a man had been successful, some would conclude, "Behind every successful man is a woman." With maturity, viewing the folly of male chauvinism, I have amended that statement: *"Beside* every successful man, one finds a wise, supportive, loving woman." Since he is "king," it seems appropriate that a "queen" reign beside him.

Another characterization of achievement holds that "success has a million fathers, while failure is an orphan." The truth is, many will claim paternity for those who reach grand heights, while those who fail will wander about in anonymity. Let us, with intensity, examine the role of mentors in shaping protégés for later success.

1) Mentors Are Intentional Coaches

The "go big" sentiment will arise in you to the degree that you allow a wise, patient, caring, intentional person—most often one who is older and more experienced—to serve as your mentor. Like an athletic coach, that person will guide you through often perilous seas on a journey of self- and others-discovery. The guidance starts with the self and extends outward. If the best is to come from your instincts, knowledge, and limited experiences, it must be honed by a mentor willing to pour out while speaking into your life.

Not surprisingly, owing to their vast base of insight covering many subjects, reflected in a life of achievement, mentors may relish telling stories and anecdotes of authenticity with analogies and allusions to where you may be presently. "Did I ever tell you about when . . . ?" Even if you have heard it many times before, it is not beneficial if you roll your eyes at the umpteenth telling of a story. In the next iteration, he/she might divulge a critical concept for success, a vital piece of data that was omitted in earlier versions of the same narrative. Or you may have a different question at this stage in your development.

One of my mentors told a story of his college entrance experiences with such frequency that I could finish it, down to the intervention by God in providing the financial resources by which he was able to matriculate. Yet, as he explained more of the details those finances were quickly dissipated by his rash actions, almost resulting in expulsion. Indeed, if I had rudely ridiculed his telling of that story, I would have missed the greater lesson: never take the grace of God for granted through foolish, ill-considered, immature actions. Truly, many will be admitted to college; the objective involves graduation in a timely manner, always trusting in God!

Another mentor lived in a small city with five freeway off-ramps. He advised me of his daily routine: take a different off-ramp, as something new in his town might escape his notice if he took the same route. That little nugget better helped me to assess my choices. Even with five options, you should celebrate multiple options, as life is never a closed world. Instead, by your choices you bring adventure to what some perceive as limited vistas.

Moreover, there are far-reaching implications of having a good mentor that stretches the parameters of your imagination. By intention, they upset preconceived notions. Let me tell of a vivid reminder of this mental stretching.

One day while in an upscale restaurant, I wanted to order dessert after my meal. So I did what people do—I inquired of my dessert options. The waiter told me. None sounded delightful to my tastes. I then proceeded to tell the waiter what I wanted for dessert, instead of accepting the presented options. He consented. When it was prepared, he brought it to my table, saying, "That came out nicely; I think I will order it that way the next time." Perhaps, the reason I felt comfortable creating my own dessert is that, three decades ago, I came under the influence of a mentor who encouraged me to think outside the box before the phrase gained traction in the larger culture.

2) Mentors Make Statements that Linger with You

As I muse on this topic, I am reminded of a beloved mentor. Out of the blue, one day he started a conversation with me regarding personal economics. I recall his encouraging me to start a pension plan. I was in my early twenties. He explained that, with compounded interest in the right financial instrument, by the time I was in my early sixties, I could retire with few worries. (I wish I could say that I took that advice then, though I have a retirement plan now.) Interestingly, I had not inquired as to the best way to plan for the future. Instead, he cared enough about me to offer advice on a sensitive subject which, had I followed it, I would have been quite secure in my finances. What is the lesson here? Good mentors take the initiative in raising issues with protégés, far beyond merely responding to questions. Mentors, in the main, do not wait for direct questions because many younger persons are too engaged in living, without principles to even know what questions to ask, as the future seems so far away.

3) Other Benefits of Mentors

Among an array of benefits from mentors, you should view their ability to push protégés beyond the safe but stultifying island of small agendas, trite rules, and frivolous pursuits while relying upon traditional reasoning. You need respected figures in your life, ones willing to shake your assumptions to their core. They should irritate and bother you to the point of strenuously evaluating where you want to go, along with the necessary steps to get there. If mentors such as teachers, pastors, supervisors, or some other experienced hand do not push you to the point of exasperation, they are not living up to their billing in your life. They should be friendly, yes, but, not your friend.

You should really think the matter through: If you are satisfied with your present position, feeling you have optimized your potential, it is not crucial to consult anyone else. Unfortunately, in such analyses, you find the formula for "go home" rather than "go big." You should loathe the former, while you love the latter.

But if you sense that another level of achievement awaits, that another dimension of attainment lies before you, that you can ascend the ladder, that a better life is possible for you, then, by all means, reach out to others.

A further benefit of mentors is their ability to impart unvarnished advice to you regarding a world of unknown challenges. Yet, you derive strength amid those challenges because you can use your mentor's pain, tears, and struggles in a vicarious manner: You obtain rewards without the travails.

In the give-and-take mentor-protégé relationship, mentors help protégés find their niche in life amid a multitude of options, some of which conflict with one another. Knowing what you may be temperamentally suited for and, conversely, not equipped for, becomes an objective exercise. Most of us are too narcissistic; we can't self-evaluate, so we try to master all things. (In the interest of full disclosure: Daily, I long to see my strengths and my weaknesses in the best light. I confess that I remain a work in progress, in the gracious hand of God.)

What I rejoice in having learned from mentors, however, is the importance of delegating responsibilities wherever possible, while holding others accountable for their actions in a timely, professional manner.

4) Mentors Represent a Picture of Your Aspirations

The best mentors are those you identify as being in places to which you aspire to go. Once a connection is made, you must avail yourself of their schedule, their inclination, and their idiosyncrasies, recognizing all you have to gain from their storehouse of knowledge, wisdom, insight, perception, expertise, experience, suffering, slights, and general accumulation of life skills. In the unfolding of the professional relationship, you will discover layers of wisdom in mentors often just waiting to be tapped. In the process, also, you will discover what you need for success.

On the other hand, mentors may not represent actual people you know. In fact, they may be persons you admire from afar. Let me tell of one. In 1992, billionaire businessman Ross Perot ran for the presidency of the United States as an Independent. I never personally met the man, but I voted for him because I felt that, as a billionaire, he couldn't be corrupted by big-money interests or corporate lobbyists.

I still remember a homespun refrain Perot repeated in a Texas twang: "Measure twice, cut once." That pithy statement, if followed, would bless millions. Often, people speed off without fully comprehending the task before them; later, sadly, they will have to "cut" twice, or more! The moral of that counsel: you should thoroughly turn a matter over in your mind before engaging action. Then, once you are aware of all your options, go for it!

5) Mentors Epitomize Excellence in Various Ways

In researching a previous book on excellence I learned that, contrary to conventional thinking, excellence is not the same as perfection. You may be tempted to avoid excellence, viewing it as an unattainable goal. In truth, however, you should view excellence as the recognition and evaluation of qualitative difference. It should be your goal to integrate noble objectives (charitable giving, ending injustice, graduation, marriage, professional success, financial security, purchasing a home, reaching political office, realization of personal dreams) with the best tools (preparation, attention to details, flair, style, dynamism, substance, written assertions, professionalism, punctuality, going further than the norm, accountability to self and others, integrity, timeliness) for reaching your stated goals.

In a world too often satisfied with sameness, trivial, mediocre, average, good-enough, or a "whatever" attitude, I encourage you toward a rendezvous with excellence. For some, excellence remains a dream, but you really need a dream to sustain your existence.

Let me share a poem by one of my longtime, insightful brothers in Christ, Evangelist Manuel Scott Jr. Its title sums up its potent content: "Dreams Keep Us Alive" (*Manuel Scott Jr. Ministries, Inc. Newsletter*, Volume 11, Issue 10).

I saw a man die today
Not from age or sickness or fright
He simply abandoned his affair with dreams
And that nailed

I mean nailed
His coffin shut

I saw a host of ghosts today
Lurking in the graveyard of routine
For they all agreed to gulp the same poison
For they all turned their backs on their dreams

For to kill a dream is to kill a life
It is to invite Death to reign from the inside
I know it takes courage
To see what can be
But
My friend
It is our Dreams
That keep us alive.

Yes, intentional mentors can be useful in capturing, nurturing, and fostering your dreams. When you discover the right mentor, you discover latent dreams. In the gracious work of God, mentors appear at critical intersections, as personal strength is depleted, to help you bring your dreams to fruition.

While seeking to make my way in the world, I aspired for success. In my mind, that meant speaking, dressing, grooming, and comporting myself as the professional I esteemed as valuable to civil society. To this day, I usually wear a dark suit to my pastoral office. In addition, a professional man should wear shined shoes. That's my rule. (When I intentionally wear jeans and a sweater with casual shoes, members make light of the ensemble, asking if I may be sick!)

In this professional dressing module, I cannot recall consciously asking any man to help me reach that goal. Instead, I found mentors who epitomized the look, the class, the elegance, the style I wanted to project, and then imitated that sartorial aesthetic. Also, magazines and newspapers I read featured corporate titans, attorneys, journalists, judges, politicians, thought leaders, and others who regularly represent themselves before the public. At the same time, if asked today, I try to convey that professional way to others, notably men of dignity, distinction, and destiny seeking to make a discernible difference in the world!

6) Mentors Inspire and Inform You of Possibilities

As mentors represent persons of indisputable achievement, they are consummate professionals, having reached a stage and age that accords with security, gravitas, integrity, dignity, and wisdom. So as they dispense principles and pragmatism, for professional and personal attainment, you should greedily absorb information and insight as an eager protégé.

Much of the indispensable in life is "caught" rather than "taught." So it behooves you to identify a mentor; then, remain in their presence as nuggets of wisdom are bound to fall from their lips. You will be immeasurably blessed by such seemingly random encounters.

7) Mentors Won't Seek You; You Must Seek Them

Men and women of singular achievement (mentors) are quite active, busy, involved, and still, figuratively, climbing new mountains. Accordingly, you must search them out. Then, you should arrange an appointment with that person. If you present sincerity regarding a clearly defined venture, most often I've found that a distinguished mentor will grant you some of his/her valuable time.

Consider yourself wise if you commit to learning from the accumulated experiences of others (mentors) without all of their hurt and pain. You can lift life lessons from what some older person went through on his/her way toward sustained achievement. Relentlessly ask that achiever about the path toward his/her success, including the drawbacks and pitfalls.

8) The Correction of a Mentor Will Save You from Headache/Heartache

By no means should you expect a mentor to function as your friend. A mentor will rarely please you; they are available to guide, correct, and facilitate your progress. Often, friends shy away from correction because as peers, they are yet struggling with the demands of success.

On the contrary, mentors, by the very measure of their age and stage of life, are secure in their careers. Mentors speak to their protégés with compassion, even if it means confrontation regarding a small infraction. They know that your one small mistake, one small moment of folly, can become the anvil of failure.

Therefore, I would recommend that you celebrate the counsel of a mentor, especially those warnings of impending danger. Relish the mentor who points out pitfalls among your peers, perspectives, use of time, preferences, values, and more.

Conclusion

After assessing (thoroughly, though not exhaustively) various aspects of the theme of unusual achievement under the rubric of chapters of this "go big" thesis, I am left with many concerns. First, will these insights be truly applied by those who yearn for more but are unsure as to where to begin? Second, are the multiple chapter headings applicable for the twenty-first-century world? Third, what might still hinder the achievement trajectory of those who can sense better, while it continually eludes them?

Princeton professor Robert P. George captures my heartfelt concerns, primarily addressing university students:

> Making the most of these years requires cultivating and practicing certain virtues, including dispassion, intellectual humility, openness of mind and, above all, love of truth. Your willingness to listen attentively and respectfully to intelligent people who challenge your beliefs, who represent causes you disagree with and points of view you do not share, will allow you to strengthen these virtues.

That 12/19/16 *Wall Street Journal* editorial, while culled from the academy, serves all persons, especially so in our world of political correctness. Let more people agree to disagree in pursuit of the way forward.

Further, I recently ran across a book written by a former twenty-year CIA analyst. In the book, he critiqued that bureaucracy for its tendency toward dogmatism, group-think, and affirming established ways of thinking. In his view, if the White House wanted a particular conclusion, the CIA was all too willing to provide the intellectual infrastructure for it. In his experience, the Iraq debacle (searching for nonexistent weapons of mass destruction) was a prime example of failure to examine suppositions.

While we may never capture the full complement of those who will steadfastly remain on the path of the "go big" ethos, perhaps we have stimulated your heart and mind as you want more from life, as reflective of your divine opportunity. I speak to your belief that the grace of God, good health, hard work, and seizing all opportunities represents your best route to sustained success.

That little phrase, "sustained success," was my motivation in writing. I sense that you are not of the flash-in-the-pan, one-hit-wonder variety of achiever. Instead, I encourage you toward a long, productive, ever-increasing life of fulfillment and attainment, constantly advancing worthy causes.

Moreover, some supra-achievers cited in this book may have lived as atheists, agnostics, cynics, and scoffers of the spiritual dimension. I cannot determine anyone's faith response to God. (I know, however, that I cannot live apart from my daily connection with my heavenly Father, made possible by repentance, acceptance, and confession of Jesus Christ as Savior and Lord). What I could do (and valiantly aspired to do) was to examine what made them respected, known, and acclaimed in their fields of endeavor.

As I give further reflection upon my initial premise that all who apply the foregoing principles will arrive at the "go big" mindset, I am reminded of millions of blacks who ventured from the American South to the states of the North and the West (the "Black Migration" well chronicled by Isabel Wilkerson). Interestingly, millions of other blacks stayed in their states of origin, with different ramifications for each group. Or I wonder, how is it two siblings may have different desires for success? Or, how is it that two friends from the same urban, tough, blighted neighborhood might choose different paths in life? When friends tell me that not all persons desire the same things (education, professionalism, material benefits, major impact), it seems an arbitrary assessment. I want to probe the matter deeper.

Perhaps it is sad but true that no matter the inducements, some will relish the safety of the familiar. My view is a different one: most satisfied with average or meager simply were not exposed to more, shown more, not mentored, nor challenged toward more, so they accepted limitations. Yet, as a spiritual merchant of change, I cannot sit idly by while people around me accept less than their best. Indeed, I sense my calling from God as a minister of the Gospel of Jesus Christ as intentionally promoting a better life, a productive life, a rich life, for you as you embrace the One who uttered words of exhortation: "I came that they may have life, and have *it* abundantly" (John 10:10b).

In summation, the foregoing chapters were my best effort to call you as world citizens to elevate your eyes, enhance your perceptions, and enlarge your capacities to dream, to focus, to organize, and to discipline yourself to walk into the brilliance of your tomorrow with faith in God and yourself. Indeed, by all means, you must "go big!"

Bibliography

The following books, articles, and materials were particularly beneficial to developing the thesis of this book. Furthering the interests of accuracy, statistics, verifiable data, versatility, eclecticism, insight, historical allusions, anecdotes, and illustrations, I read widely.

Particularly, I draw references from many daily newspapers: *The New York Times*, *Wall Street Journal*, *USA Today*, *Washington Post*, *Kansas City Star*, and *Los Angeles Times*.

Favored periodicals include *Newsweek*, *Time*, *Atlantic Monthly*, *The New Yorker*, *Harvard Business Review*, *US News & World Report*, *The Economist*, *Black Enterprise*, *Success*, *The Robb Report*, and more.

The following books were also important in framing the parameters of my thesis:

Anaybwile, Thabiti. *Reviving the Black Church*. Nashville, TN: B & H Publishing Group, 2015.

Begg, Alistair. *The Hand of God*. Chicago, IL: Moody Press, 1999.

Bennett, William J. *The Book of Virtues*. New York, NY: Simon & Schuster, 1993.

Foreman, George. *Going the Extra Smile*. Nashville, TN: Thomas Nelson, 2007.

Franklin, Robert M. *Crisis in the Village*. Minneapolis, MN: Fortress Press, 2007.

Gladwell, Malcolm. *David and Goliath*. New York, NY: Little, Brown and Company, 2013.

Hamilton, Adam. *Leading beyond the Walls*. Nashville, TN: Abingdon Press, 2002.

Labberton, Mark. *Called*. Downers Grove, IL: InterVarsity Press, 2014.

MacDonald, Gordon. *Building below the Waterline*. Peabody, MA: Hendrickson Publishers, 2011.

Niebuhr, H. Richard. *Christ and Culture*. New York, NY: Harper & Row, 1951.

Orman, Greg. *A Declaration of Independents*. Austin, TX: Greenleaf Book Group Press, 2016.

Patterson, A. Louis, Jr. *Joy for the Journey*. Lithonia, GA: Ornan Press, 2002.

Perry, Steve. *Push Has Come to Shove*. New York, NY: Broadway Paperbacks, 2011.

Proctor, Samuel D. *The Certain Sound of the Trumpet*. Valley Forge, PA: Judson Press, 1994.

Proctor, Samuel D., and Gardner C. Taylor. *We Have This Ministry*. Valley Forge, PA: Judson Press, 1996.

Rainer, Thomas S. *Who Moved My Pulpit?* Nashville, TN: B & H Publishing Group, 2016.

Sanders, Richard D., and Candace Cole Kelly. *In His Hands*. Nashville, TN: Townsend Press, 2015.

Smiley, Tavis, and Cornel West. *The Rich and the Rest of Us*. New York, NY: SmileyBooks, 2012.

Wilkerson, Isabel. *The Warmth of Other Suns*. New York, NY: Knopf Doubleday Publishing, 2010.

www.ingramcontent.com/pod-product-compliance
Lightning Source LLC
Chambersburg PA
CBHW071615080526
44588CB00010B/1143